Machiavelli's Children

Edward Pearce is one of Britain's most distinguished political commentators. He writes regularly for the *Guardian* and the *New Statesman*, and also for the *Daily Mail*, *Literary Review* and *London Review of Books*. He is a panellist on BBC TV's *The Moral Maze* and has published seven books since 1982.

Born in the Midlands, raised in the North, educated in Oxford and Sweden, Edward Pearce lives in Buckinghamshire.

Machiavelli's Children

EDWARD PEARCE

VICTOR GOLLANCZ

LONDON

First published in Great Britain 1993
by Victor Gollancz

First Gollancz Paperback edition published 1995
by Victor Gollancz
An imprint of the Cassell Group
Wellington House, 125 Strand, London WC2R 0BB

A catalogue record for this book is
available from the British Library.

ISBN 0 575 05798 X

Printed and bound in Great Britain
by Guernsey Press Co. Ltd, Guernsey, Channel Isles

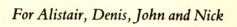
For Alistair, Denis, John and Nick

Contents

Introduction   *page* 9

CHAPTER ONE   13
Settlements do not cost much: France and colonial Algeria
(*The Prince* III)

CHAPTER TWO   26
*In order to enter a country one needs the goodwill of its
inhabitants*: General Sharon makes peace in the Lebanon
(*The Prince* III)

CHAPTER THREE   44
The Overzealous Lieutenant: Mrs Thatcher
ignores Machiavelli and cherishes three of them
(*The Prince* VII)

CHAPTER FOUR   62
Those who come to power by crime: The rise and fall of
Captain Röhm
(*The Prince* VIII)

CHAPTER FIVE   71
Further and better *coming to power by crime*: The
exploding star of Bashir Gemayel
(*The Prince* VIII)

CHAPTER SIX A   86
The Prophet Unarmed: The high regard for legal
means of General Charles de Gaulle in 1958
(*The Prince* IX)

CHAPTER SIX B   106
The Prophet Armed: The delicate exercise of
power by General Charles de Gaulle after 1958
(*The Prince* IX)

CHAPTER SEVEN   120
How a prince should organize his militia: The NKVD
and the SS compared and contrasted
(*The Prince* XIV)

CHAPTER EIGHT   139
Generosity and parsimony; Cruelty and compassion:
Thoughts in passing on Kennedy and Khrushchev, but,
chiefly, the expensive, effective career of Juan Domingo
Perón
(*The Prince* XVI and XVII)

CHAPTER NINE   160
How princes should honour their word: The frugal
gratitude of General Francisco Franco
(*The Prince* XVIII)

CHAPTER TEN   168
The need to avoid contempt and hatred: How Benito
Mussolini was loved until he was hated
(*The Prince* XIX)

CHAPTER ELEVEN   185
How a prince must act to win honour: President George
Bush and his followers in the Gulf War
(*The Prince* XXI)

CHAPTER TWELVE   198
A prince's personal staff and *How flatterers must be shunned*:
The contrasted experience of Harold Wilson and Margaret
Thatcher
(*The Prince* XXII and XXIII)

Bibliography   218

ACKNOWLEDGEMENTS

I would like to express sincere thanks to Tony Rilett, computer software specialist who has made writing *Machiavelli's Children* possible on a machine cleverer than I am, Liz Knights of Gollancz who has edited with tact and consideration and my wife, Deanna, who has helped at every corner.

EP

INTRODUCTION

Niccolò Machiavelli is one of the few certain pleasures of the politics syllabus. At a time when most academics speak a horrid jargon, he speaks plain. In a trade full of moral cowardice expressed in language apt for cowardice, he is heroically, almost crazily, direct. He confronts the schemes, frauds and crimes of politicians by calling them that, but not in order to preach against them. His message is that if you want something, then to do this and this are the best ways of getting it. If you find this and this offensive and wrong, don't do them, but don't expect the prize you sought, either.

For such candour he was, for centuries, denounced from the pulpits of all churches; his surname was attached to hyperintelligent villainy, his first name was linked to the Devil. It would be better to see Machiavelli as the godfather of candour, as the stripper-off of polite forms (there is very little tease); the man who observes Ferdinand of Aragon cheating and remarks how well it served him, and who gave us the armed man certain to assume command over the unarmed. If such observation sometimes involves him, as critics say, in banality, it is an unacknowledged banality; he affords a recognition of truths rarely uttered and commonly flinched from. But although *The Prince* is a magnificent textbook, we should not forget that its author lived in an actual world. He was a citizen of Florence, one of its ambassadors, a witness of the exercise of Medici and papal power and, ironically, a rather unsuccessful politician who suffered torture and imprisonment.

His friend Francesco Guicciardini, to whom I allude in this work, was an altogether more successful politician in terms of office held. But both men shared the humiliation of seeing their ambition for a united Italy recede and the petty particularism of fraction-states intensify. Both, to the end of a greater Italy, put their talents at the service of charmless despots. Machiavelli, even with his devotion to Cesare Borgia, showed better judgement than his friend who ended up working for Alessandro de' Medici, a psychopath with the potential of Caligula.

Even so, sixteenth-century politics in its roughest forms – here a garrotting, there a *strappado*, with the odd assassination thrown in – was, for all its brutal assumptions, a mere play-ground compared with our own murderous century. But the rules haven't changed. Things done by Hitler and Stalin and by small-time killers like Bashir Gemayel in the Lebanon are done with a ferocious grasp of means and contempt for things and people standing in the way that recall the hard men of the late Renaissance. In the kinder, gentler world of Margaret Thatcher and General de Gaulle (not names naturally coupled), the same rules and requirements apply, but the blood which flows is symbolic. It was more real, however, during the Gulf War which, in connection with the name of President George Bush, is examined here in the light of Machiavelli's comments upon what a prince must do to enjoy honour.

Most of Machiavelli's assumptions hold true. The over-zealous lieutenant is a natural fall-guy for a chief who wishes to resile from a strategy which has made too many enemies. The armed man prevails over his unarmed neighbours. Fear works better than gratitude. The statesman must be both lion to inspire respect and fox to avoid traps.

But Machiavelli himself illustrates his precepts from either the history of his times or that Roman and Greek history, once the central strand of a common civilization, which now lies at the margin of antiquarianism. University students are delightful people, but the Secretary for Education is right. Their education has left them encyclopaedically uninformed. Not only will they never have heard of such Machiavelli examples as Oliverotto of Fermo or Agathocles the Sicilian, but I would not even put money on their having heard of Cesare Borgia. As for Alexander the Great, he probably looms up vaguely in the same blur as Julius Caesar. If anyone is inclined to dispute this, I refer him to the member of Mrs Thatcher's cabinet who, when I suggested to him a parallel between his own current actions and the hard fate of a character in *The Prince*, replied 'Oh, Machiavelli's *Prince*, I haven't read that. It's a great long book, isn't it?'

So – a little for amusement, more to be helpful in grasping Machiavelli, but never, please, to be 'relevant', the most hellish word in all academic patter – I have set about illustrating *The Prince* for students and general readers with examples drawn from our own times, from the lives and acts of *inter alia* Ernst Röhm, Francisco Franco, Juan Domingo Perón, Harold Wilson and Joseph Stalin. The familiar lessons of politics are here, occasionally disputed as with Perón's successful application of largess, occasionally told by inversion as with Mrs Thatcher's failure to shift blame for the calamitous poll tax upon any of three ardently willing lieutenants.

But Machiavelli's precept is still asserted, even though the examples come from our time. Machiavelli will always be pertinent as long as men itch for power. The purpose of this book is to demonstrate his truths from different lives in another age. It serves, I believe, an enlightening purpose and is meant to arouse interest in the study of politics and provoke contemplation of the seamless ferocity of men in power. As such an undertaking, I commend it in hope.

CHAPTER ONE

Settlements do not cost much: France and colonial Algeria

(*The Prince* III)

The case is made by Machiavelli, with some insistence, in his own third chapter that settlements in a captive territory are a 'superior expedient' for the conqueror. Such settlements will, as it were,

> fetter the state for you. Unless you establish settlements, you will have to garrison large numbers of mounted troops and infantry. Settlements do not cost much and the prince can found them and maintain them at little or no personal expense. He injures only those from whom he takes land and houses to give to the new inhabitants and these form a tiny minority and can never do any harm since they remain poor and scattered.

Machiavelli was arguing for the *economy* of settlements, for their being less harsh and thus making fewer enemies than a military presence which humiliates, affronts and sets the local people against the intruder. His example, a very broad one without detail, is the Romans, who established settlements of former Roman soldiers with Roman citizenship and allegiance throughout their empire. The very names of places indicate as much. The city of Cologne or Köln in the Rhineland is, after all, the former Colonia.

Interestingly, when the British, French and other European powers established colonies, though they took the Roman word, they quickly imparted a different meaning to it. A colony in Rhodesia or Kenya was London's concern. However much white planters took out season-tickets on upper-class social status within the settled territory, the colonies were, though non-sovereign, thought of as entire countries, natives included. Ministries were established in Paris and London to supervise them. This may have been humbug, but it was humbug whose paper meaning could ultimately be enforced.

It was the original purpose of the Rhodesia Front party, before the breach with Britain in 1965, to have their country move away from the legal status of colony and turn their *de facto* self-government into parity with the white 'dominions'. Very roughly, in the Kipling–Salisbury–Milner world, colonies were places where white men were in practical charge of non-white men but with the bottom line drawn (and sometimes redrawn) in Paris or London. Dominions were places where the local white men were in power absolutely and in perpetuity. So empowered, the Australian immigration service, *after* the Second World War, systematically barred south Europeans as unsuitable racial types and internally memoed itself on the need for the country to be replenished with what it really did call 'Aryan stock'.

Fortunately for Machiavelli but unfortunately for his argument in the long term, he did not live through the process of decolonization; though in his text he is briskly aware of the risk to a conqueror from the hatreds of the conquered. His preference for colonists and settlements is founded on the fact that they are less hateful to the locals than a permanent military garrison. However, it became the experience of modern colonial powers that their colonies (in the Roman sense) of planters and farmers, grouped around European suburbs transplanted to central and southern Africa, were sufficiently in danger from the ungrateful conquered population making up the rest of the colony (in the modern sense), to need the support of great numbers of the military if they were to stay *in situ* or indeed alive.

The French experience in Algeria might have been shared by

the British in several colonies. But British passivity or good sense caused the UK to cut the sort of losses which France in pride, energy and rage ran up until she was on the brink of internal collapse. As examiners put it, 'Compare and contrast'!

A war not much talked of since it happened was fought in Kenya in the early fifties to preserve the fettering and securing colonists. Brutal acts of terror on the part of the Kikuyu were met by acts of no great sensibility on the part of the British. The outcome was a victory, but one of those victories that contain the germ of future defeat (to be called something else). It would have been as unimaginable to the third Marquess of Salisbury from whom the capital of Rhodesia took its name, as to Cecil Rhodes for whom the entire colony was titled, that fifty years after their heyday, Conservative politicians should be broadly agreed on the need to liquidate colonies and dispose of settlements by brushing aside the settlers in favour of native peoples. By that time the British had resolved to lose – that is to say they gave up and went away, which is as good a definition of losing as any.

The decision may have owed a very little to high-mindedness, the exertions of Hugh Foot in Cyprus being a case in point. But high-mindedness is not precisely a force in history, though it may be an interesting means of debilitation. High-mindedness is an alibi, placed to the front when motives preferring not to speak their name predominate. Essentially the European nations got out of their colonial empires for three clear reasons: fear of Communism, deference to the United States and shortage of money. The exact utility of Marxism in territories with perhaps seventy years of plantation economics behind them was never clear. But my enemy's enemy has always seemed like a good chap, and reference to him has startling effects. Kikuyu terrorist leaders gave themselves names like 'General China' and 'General Russia'. As statements these were worthless but effective – the conquered natives' equivalent to the handful of glass beads proffered by settlers. The British exhibited both the general paranoia about Soviet intentions and a perfectly sensible apprehension that the Soviets aimed to pick up what they could get and were likely to make trouble to that end.

The Americans, under the foreign policy directorate of John Foster Dulles, a man of spectacular unfitness to engage in a world which he did not understand but was mightily dogmatic about, had the same fears in all suits. But the Americans, who tended not to have read Machiavelli, or anything very much, preferred to handle backward or dependent territories not by means of settlements but by using local élites, with a special predilection for the local criminal community. The Somoza clan, or in Sicily a somewhat more extensive family, seemed better bets than any cliques of coffee-planters or sisal-growers.

It was the peculiar genius of Dulles to unite a taste for low life in South American government – such a company of assassins, protection racketeers, gold-frogged military parasites and drug-traffickers as the world can hardly imagine – with a piety of the relentless and broadcast sort, scarcely drawing breath in its discontent with the moral insufficiencies of other men. Upon the colony-keeping British such sentiments were recurringly wreaked. Now it has been the fate of Britain in all international undertakings since at least the forties to play *vis-à-vis* the United States the role of the parrot on the shoulder of Long John Silver. To this condition it was brought by the 'need for a world role', a craving no more explicable than capable of fulfilment. We were broke and infatuated. There were good reasons for giving up colonies, not least the colonists. But we left because we had lost, even if we didn't admit to losing.

Nevertheless we did go from the great majority of our colonies in very short order. Once the decision had been made, we precipitately thrust sovereignty, a parliamentary mace and a copy of *Citrine on Chairmanship*, together with a royal visit and words of inexpressible (and unbankable) goodwill, upon more overseas territories than you could shake a stick at. This was essentially the doing of the Macmillan government, executed by Iain Macleod, an ambitious, able, witty, emotionally brutal, partisan politician and above everything else a gamester. He was literally so – an *habitué* of bridge clubs where he augmented his income and was twice warned off for the gaming crime of deliberately engaging with players of lesser skills. Macleod is remembered in some circles as a liberal on social matters, and this was not untrue, but he was supremely a short-term combat politician preoccupied with action.

His chief, Harold Macmillan, is best seen as the arch-apostle of despair. Macmillan also had generous and humane instincts; he had fought in the first war, commanding working men in uniform. He had later been MP for Stockton in South Durham throughout the depression. The effect of all this had been to make him pessimistic and demoralized. He did not fundamentally believe in the order he was charged with defending. To the Tory right Macmillan was a simple betrayer of the Empire. To others, he was a wise pre-empter of hopeless struggle and a humane and merciful presence.

Machiavelli would have been more fascinated by him than by any other British politician of the last fifty years. *The Prince* was written under the shadow of Cesare Borgia's driving ambition to create an Italian kingdom and thus expresses an optimistic spirit. It is a book about winning. Macmillan, who thought in terms of things lasting for our time, would have irked the Florentine. However, his finesse in abandoning obligations with no more fuss than a little pat on his own back would surely have aroused professional admiration.

When it came to the interests of colonial settlements, Macmillan, like the idle wind, regarded them not. The perplexities which would come to France and threaten the entire state did not come to us. Macmillan was able in Kenya to work through a sympathetic settler, Michael Blundell, who as chief minister negotiated, less than ten years after the ending of the Mau Mau emergency, an independence which gave power to Jomo Kenyatta, the moving spirit of Mau Mau. The fettering and securing settlement was deftly eased from its fetters and left unsecured to anything except an independent black African future.

Settlers reacted by throwing thirty small coins at Blundell in the traditional (and banal) Judas insult. But a central principle of betrayal, with which Machiavelli would surely have concurred, is to betray only those unable to do anything in response except complain. Two hundred and forty thousand whites in Rhodesia were able to make more trouble for the central authority, but not enough to save themselves. And the war they fought against African opponents was at their expense and loss of life, not Britain's.

The guiding premise of Macmillan's decolonization policy was that the territory that had been taken could not be kept except at an exorbitant cost in blood and money. This premise was linked to a premonitory judgement, in which his profound pessimism proved right, that modern wars would lack the cheerfully gallant image of remote campaigns reported in small type ten days late. All wars benefit from a blurred focus and cursory attention, or from jogging along at a steady pace to which the voters are attuned. This last would prove possible in Northern Ireland. In Vietnam it did not, with disturbing and divisive consequences for the United States which had engaged there. Vietnam had no settlers, only the sort of commitment created by native allies. The United States was fettered and secured by colonial chains without the pleasures of a colony. In the local Vietnamese the Americans had confected their own settlement.

To Americans bitterly at odds, abusing one another, according to taste as traitors or war criminals, the charm of Harold Macmillan's gentlemanly disobligation of British settlers in Africa now looked like elemental wisdom. His own *sotto voce* observation about playing Greeks to the American Romans seemed at this point to have been entirely in order. We had, at any rate, a name for realism developed to the point of raffish perfidy. Even in the autumn of 1992, Mr Bush would assault

[18]

Mr Clinton for the pernicious influence, Hellenic or Levantine, of Oxford and England upon his moral character.

But the supreme example of an unbetrayed settlement so fettering the colonial power as to drag it under water and well-nigh drown it was Algeria. That country had been won by French arms in 1830 and had been established, in the florid, assertive way of French public policy, not as a colony but as an integral province of metropolitan France, 'as much part of France', they said, 'as Lot-et-Garonne'. Accordingly, Algeria had been settled with Frenchmen. Following the Roman example, these *colons* were French citizens rather than necessarily natives of French soil.

There were large numbers of Italians, Corsicans (very un-French and nasty with it) and Jews; but they voted in French elections and constituted a *département*. They were also very numerous by the standards of settlements, 10 per cent of the total population: fettering indeed, with heavy irons. So much were the settlers part of France that, during the period of German conquest and of the collaborationist Vichy government, the French of Algeria were inclined to go merrily along with Hitler, just like most of France. But Algeria was not taken by the Germans and eventually, after the assassination of the collaborationist Admiral Darlan, Algiers served, not terribly happily, as headquarters for de Gaulle and the Free French.

There also existed in Algeria the Algerians. In 1945 a killing of a hundred *colons* was followed by the killing of some six thousand Arabs. This pattern would recur until France, preoccupied post-war by many things, finally appreciated that a full-scale war of independence was being fought. The possibility of conciliation, of integrating *colon* and Arab, which had been urged by liberal governors before the war and immediately after, had been lost. Maurice Violette, one of those decent men, had seen what was coming: 'As long as thirty years ago I said that if the Muslims of Algeria were not given a square deal, they would take the law into their own hands.' He was 'haunted by the thought of what is to happen to both France and Algeria'.

What had already happened was the involvement of the military – precisely the people that Machiavelli had wished to keep out of conquered territory because, he said, they made unnecessary enemies. The military were not casual brutes; their senior officers frequently had warm feelings towards the Muslim population. But in ways which invert Machiavelli's thinking, they came rapidly to believe that without Algeria 'France would cease to be a power'. Instead of lands enhancing the holder, here they obliged and defined him. The pleasing addition to one's territory, to be firmly subjected and then looked after by a settlement of colonists owing everything to the central power, had been replaced with a cross held by birthright. The notion of defeat in Algeria was compared to Sedan.

Sedan, the decisive defeat at Prussian hands in 1870, marked the end of the Napoleonic notion of France as the leading military nation of Europe. It was a hang-up which had made France half-psychotic for three generations. A colonial loss that might have such impact had exceeded Renaissance notions of territorial value. It had done so because public politics – democratic politics as we like to call it – had created pressures and emotions less cynically discountable than the changing whims of an absolute ruler. Single rulers are mad enough, but they are commonly outrun in emotional distress by popular fury.

Trying to save the Algeria without which France would cease to exist, and shocked by rebel savagery – much cutting-up and cutting-off – the army began extensively, indeed as a matter of routine, to use torture. So did Renaissance princes, for pleasure or use; but they were not troubled by the other sort of public opinion, the liberal kind that takes moral exception to administrative unpleasantness. A Machiavellian prince would have minded less about losing a colony, but would also have acted as cruelly as his own stomach would bear. Nobody would have sat on one shoulder telling him never to lose the territory, or on the other telling him to behave decently. The successful operation of colonies requires a certain lightness of heart.

Certainly such a prince would never have been a prisoner of the settlements which one may 'establish at little cost'. Successive French governments from the early fifties onwards found themselves morally obliged to the settlers, whose wholesale murder was threatened, but also afraid of them, because the rage and malevolence of the *colons* was hard for rational metropolitan men to cope with. Ministers deferred to the military who believed in victory and kept talking about '*le dernier quart d'heure*' (about three hours of them). And they came eventually to be afraid of the army which had the means, and the slow-stirring inclination, to effect a coup d'état. For the whole of this period during which France was preoccupied by the question of a colony she was, by elegant paradox, in greatest danger of falling into the pattern of a South American country, an Argentina or Bolivia; in her colonial preoccupation, she began to behave like a former colony.

The pressure reached a plateau of intensity early in 1956 when the newly elected Prime Minister, Guy Mollet, went to Algiers. General Catroux, Mollet's choice for governor-general, though elderly, was another liberal; the intentions of the Socialist government, though imprecise, were not unsympathetic to the Arabs.

The French *colons*, stirred up by France's indigenous, worse-than-Fascist right wing, simply threw things. They had been told by one Biaggi, an influential local Gaullist, that 'We must raise the temperature and bring down the regime . . . the Fifth Republic must arise from the street . . . The Fourth has had it'.

The throwing came when Mollet visited Algiers and went to lay a wreath on the war memorial. He did so to a hail of tomatoes, oranges and torn-up tufts of lawn accompanied by cries of 'Hang Catroux' and, a phrase to be heard again, '*Algérie française*'. The 'Marseillaise' itself was shouted down by these patriots. Steel-helmeted troops were present, and though commandos under the orders of General Jacques Massu cleared the rioters away and gave the Prime Minister protection, the ambiguity of the military – whom the settlers were to have made unnecessary and who could now so easily be the sword of the settlers – will have occurred to Mollet. General Massu kept on his desk around this time one book, a copy of *Counter-revolution, Strategy and Tactics*.

Meanwhile Mollet had been told by the Prefect of Algiers that safety could not be guaranteed to Georges Catroux if he came in person to the capital of the province he was intended to govern. Back in France, Catroux offered his resignation. It was accepted. Mollet had a brave and honourable record in the Resistance but, as so often, physical courage was not matched by moral courage: in this case, the courage to face down blind, vituperative rage. There followed, against the first wishes of the government and its natural supporters on the left, a sustained period of repression. In Robert Lacoste, a fellow Socialist who took the side of the small-time whites against the rich whites (and the blacks), Mollet found an executive officer highly acceptable to the settlement. There had been talk of reducing military commitment in Algeria. Instead, 70,000 reservists were recalled and the number of troops in Algeria increased from 200,000 to 400,000. But the fighting of the war, so far from strengthening the army's ties to government, produced discontents, apprehension of betrayal and much loose and not–so–loose talk of treason.

The situation also propelled France towards another war. Egypt, not surprisingly, was sympathetic to the Algerian revolutionary force (FLN) and was in some measure a supplier of arms to it; she was also a great maker of windy radio denunciations of France, which France, with equal pomposity, took seriously. The French mood after the nationalization of the Suez canal differed from the British one of widespread resistance to war, which had involved the major and minor opposition parties and a great, oddly French, manifestation of public protest in Trafalgar Square. French opposition to war was minimal, confined (apart from the Communists) to a small circle around

Pierre Mendès-France, a politician of rugged, inveterate conscience by whom Machiavelli would have been perplexed. France was primed for the Suez war because of her prior involvement in a North African conflict.

Algeria and its settlement had made her a bristling little soldier. 'One division in Egypt', said Robert Lacoste, 'is worth four divisions in Algeria.' In the words of Frank Giles, most temperate chronicler of these times, 'War against Egypt satisfied the deepest cravings of the French soul at that moment.' The soul has its uses but they should not include the initiation of foreign and military policy. Intimate commitment to a colony and identification of its retention with national glory made France dance to the tune of a million or so rather unengaging settlers led by froth-bubbling zealots – indeed, made France interestingly mad. (Anthony Eden, who had involved Britain in the same scrape, was, after all, at the time, the victim of a severed bile-duct and physiologically disordered in ways that brought him close to derangement.)

Sincerity is a dangerous thing, since sincerity ignores calculation of self-interest in favour of empty proclamation of right. At this time, France was as far from Florentine thinking as could be; France was shaking a fist at the moon. Meanwhile, after the humiliation of withdrawal from Suez, imposed upon Britain and thus on France by the United States, the real war continued. The war against the FLN outlasted the governments of Mollet, Maurice Bourgès-Maunoury, Félix Gaillard and others, its progress encompassing the end of the Fourth Republic, about which the febrile Maître Biaggi had been prescient.

The war was conducted by people like General Jacques Massu and it took the name of pacification. There was a creditable side to pacification. The blue-capped special administrative sections worked in Arab villages, led by men who spoke the language and ran parts of the country sympathetically and rather well. Pacification will be remembered, however, as the battle of Algiers. Further bombings and assassinations by the FLN (and bombings by the more lively *colons*) were followed by division of

[23]

the city into squares, of which troops made sweeping searches. Torture had been well known in Algeria before, but now it became very nearly the administrative norm. Although it also included water-dousing, cigarette burns and simple repeated punching in the face, torture chiefly took the form of electricity – electricity attached to the nostril, mouth, ear, anus, penis or vagina.

Torture may be defended on grounds of expediency – with respect to hidden bombs, say – but no defence quite sustains the glory of France. The reaction that systematic demi-electrocution provoked from writers – left-wing, Catholic, and old-fashioned liberal; books by Henri Alleg (himself a victim) and Pierre-Henri Simon, articles by Jean-Jacques Servan-Schreiber and a single cool devastating newspaper column by Raymond Aron – says something for the usefulness of writers. It also illustrated the fact that France had had all her old historic wounds reopened and that she was divided, not so much between head and heart as between both those organs and the fingers used for attaching wires. As someone observed at the time, political paralysis took the form of there being in France neither a majority for pursuing the war *jusqu'au bout*, nor one for getting out of it, only for stumbling along with the status quo.

These are circumstances in which governments can offer neither peace nor victory; when to their own military and, importantly, to the settlers, they leave open the fearful possibility of pulling out of the war, and to the civilian population at home become simply inept plodders carrying war as an unending burden.

Pierre Mendès-France, who could see that the war was wrong and impossible, had said in another context '*Gouverner c'est choisir*' (to govern is to choose). So it is. Not to make choices is to occupy office, which is what the last governments of the Fourth Republic did until May 1958. Conspirators drawn from the army and the *colons*, activated by freelance but uncorrected spokesmen for General de Gaulle, made their moves. By illegal means and intimidation, treason in short, the Fourth Republic would be overthrown and General de Gaulle put in its place. The actions of the general, a convinced writer-off of *Algérie française*, in subsequently committing a sensible *trahison du soldat* and putting the settlers in their low and proper place, will appear elsewhere in this study. But that settlement, a bunch of unappetizing colonial whites, had managed in half a decade to do things not dreamed of in sixteenth century Florence.

France attended to its needs and desires. The army, initially not a little despising it, became the settlement's protector and undertook a Faustian journey of institutionalized sadism before engaging in treason against the French state. All the intelligence of France – de Gaulle, Mendès-France, Raymond Aron – understood that the brutal game was not worth the fire-hazarding candle. Lesser men in office, like Mollet himself ('I shouldn't have given in to them'), more dimly perceived as much. And yet so unworthy, so inherently contemptible a thing as this huddle of racist whites, in a country to which they had only the ties of opportunism, was to drag France to the brink of Fascism at the very time that her economy was quietly preparing for triumph.

Settlements since Machiavelli's time have lost their malleable quality, and in Northern Ireland and the Jewish-occupied West Bank such holdings have taken on a life of their own, a bigoted and unattractive life. Money-devouring, infant-imperious, noisily irrational and a threat to the main nation's stability, settlements litter the twentieth century; and those who established them have commonly wished them never settled. They may also have wished for the return of crisp, late-medieval administrative assumptions towards dependents.

Chapter Two

In order to enter a country one needs the goodwill of its inhabitants: General Sharon makes peace in the Lebanon

(*The Prince* III)

Chapter 3 of *The Prince* is fecund with imperial notions, of which settlements are just one. Machiavelli, under the heading of what he calls rather bureaucratically 'composite principalities', writes there of the invader coming into a territory where there is local division which he hopes to exploit and where he has, or tries to have, allies. He has no illusions about the motives of the allies: 'King Louis was brought into Italy by the ambition of the Venetians who wanted by this means to win for themselves half of Lombardy.'

The policy worked, as far as it went, though this king, Louis XII, would come unstuck later for different reasons. Meanwhile the neighbours recognized the force of force.

> Genoa capitulated; the Florentines became his allies; the marquis of Mantua, the duke of Ferrara, the Bentivogli, the countess of Forlì, the rulers of Faenza, of Pesaro, of Rimini, of Camerino, of Piombino, the citizens of Lucca, Pisa, Siena all came forward to seek his friendship. Then the Venetians were in a position to realize how rash they had been. In order to gain two towns in Lombardy, they had made him, the king, ruler of a third of Italy.

Machiavelli spells out the risks involved in bringing in outsiders but he then shows his king losing what he had gained and argues what a king *might* have done to retain the territory.

The Lebanon, which will serve us as the modern example of a composite principality, chopped and diced as it had been into confessional factions and sub-factions, was, in the mid-1970s, not unlike northern Italy in relation to an intervening Israel. Israel did not, it is true, wish to annexe Lebanon. Let me rephrase that: not everyone in Israel wished to annexe all Lebanon. Lebanon was a sovereign state into which had come, like a rogue hormone, the forces of the Palestine Liberation Organization. This enemy launched against Israel ineffective but decently bloody excursions. Israel at first wished only to move against the Palestinians by way of hot pursuit and short incursion. But no man, said Cromwell, goeth so far as he that knows not whither he is going. In fairness, General Ariel Sharon, Israeli Minister of Defence and practitioner of a steady brutalism in dealings with the Palestinians, had an excellent idea of where he was going; but early encountering the intense disapproval of most of the cabinet, he kept his embarrassing activities from them and, in sketchy contact with a sympathetic prime minister, Menachem Begin, struck out briskly for his objective.

Opinion was influenced in Israeli politics by the *obiter dicta* of Alexander Haig, improbably United States Secretary of State, a man of imperious caprice who expressed his bitter hostility to another party with interests in the Lebanon, the Syrians. He was against them. They were anathema for being a client state of the Soviet Union, much as Israel, for all her stroppiness, was the client of the United States. As the former dominant partner in a unitary state organized by France, Syria was far from popular with many Lebanese, especially the Maronite Christians, a minority on tiptoe whose superiority complex towards the Muslim majority in Lebanon was deemed threatened by the involvement of Muslim Syria.

The Christian Lebanese, at once Counter-Reformation Catholics, mafiosi, Arabs and fearful élite, might not be naturally at ease with the Jewish state. Their natural inheritance was a clerical-Fascist one of the French and Spanish school, their elder leaders still admirers of thirties models of European government. But they had in common with Israel an immediate on-site enemy, the PLO, which had made its way into the Lebanon with the government's unhappy consent in 1969 after the 'Black September' assault by Jordanian Bedouin troops which enabled King Hussein to regain working control of his country. And the Palestinians in the Lebanon had been behaving in the way of footloose armies of the discontented ever since.

As Machiavelli puts it, 'For always, no matter how powerful one's armies, in order to enter a country one needs the goodwill of its inhabitants.' This, after much swagger, rape and murder of citizens, the PLO did not have. Israel, as the displacer of the Palestinians and occupier of the West Bank of the Jordan, was harassed rather than threatened by the PLO. But Israel has never been a loser through overstating or overreacting to its anxieties. The getting-in of retaliation early had been raised to a fine art, including the restitution on Israeli-controlled Arab territory of what the Normans after the conquest called *Frankpledge*: the collective liability to punishment of the community in which an offence against the occupier had taken place. Shots are fired at an Israeli patrol; houses in the street where this happened are then pulled down. It is good eleventh-century thinking. But Sharon, a bully with charm and bravado, something of a Jewish Goering, went far beyond holding everything and conceding nothing. He was bent upon territorial conquest, the expunging of Palestinians from all Lebanon, the defeat and expulsion of Syria from that country and its transformation into a condominium controlled in the south by Israel and in Beirut by a proxy creature – a Maronite government in the hands of the Gemayel faction, the evocatively named Phalange. The keystone of this overarching (and overreaching) design would be

Bashir Gemayel, ablest, most cynical and flexible of the clan. Bashir, whose personal story is related in chapter five, naturally wanted power for himself. Usefully for Sharon's purposes, however, he violently opposed the Syrians backing the rival Franjieh family and was ready to work with the Israelis against Syrians and Palestinians alike. Like many men who themselves charm and deceive, Sharon was susceptible to the charm and deception of others. He came to hold Gemayel in genuine regard and affection, trusting him unwisely and investing belief in the military competence of the Phalange, a body notable mainly for cowardice modified by tribal savagery towards the unarmed. But then Sharon was like a share-pushing business-man for whom confidence in the line boosted turns into a sort of love. The line Sharon was selling – his combination of conquest, expulsions and alliance with a Gemayel-led Maronite Lebanon – had a name. In the way of an estate agent, he called it Operation Big Pines.

Israeli and Maronite interests corresponded with regard to both the Palestinians and the Syrians. Nothing that was good for Hafiz Assad, ruler of Syria, could do other than diminish Maronite influence and threaten Israel with a militarily compe-tent enemy coming from a new, wrong angle. But divisions of opinion existed in both camps. General Yehoshua Saguy, Israeli head of intelligence and a man of high professional competence and steady good sense, regarded all dealings with the Maronites as serving their ends rather than Israel's and as liable to involve an intervening Israel in remote imbroglios. He saw her being drawn into the Christians' quarrels and, since militarily the Christians were very nearly useless, doing all the fighting. There was a parallel and complementary scepticism among many of the Maronites. One of the contesting factions, the Franjieh family, a most powerful grouping, had old and sturdy links with the Syrians despite the confessional gulf, and pre-ferred that they, and not the Israelis, should be drawn into the struggle with the PLO.

Most normal Israeli thinking, however harsh, was defensive and would never have countenanced more than short incursions away-day raids, as it were. Attempts to sell Big Pines openly as candid big-dream aggression had failed – though not with Menachem Begin. The prime minister who thirty-three years before had authorized the King David Hotel mass killing was a believer in a greater Israel, and his carnivorous naïvety was ideally attuned to Sharon's thinking. But the plan had died the death with the General Staff. When Begin presented an outline of it to cabinet, General Saguy and the liberal and religious factions objected strenuously and the sketch was withdrawn.

The massive involvement which did subsequently occur was brought about by the determination and deceit of Sharon once he himself had been advanced to the post of Minister of Defence and was able not so much to win his case outright as sell it on hire-purchase. The invasion took place because General Sharon, by bluff and guile, by exploiting the goodwill of his prime minister and the nerveless, unenquiring condition of his colleagues, was to take upon himself, for a little but sufficient time, powers not signally different from those of an Italian prince of the early sixteenth century.

If Sharon's invasion of the Lebanon had been a success, Israel would have crushed her enemy, the PLO, and driven it far from Israel's *de facto* borders, would have acquired a client state under a dependent if sensationally untrustworthy leader and inflicted a major defeat upon the most respected of all her Arab opponents, Syria. She would also have achieved American goodwill by inflicting a defeat on the Soviet Union whose client Syria was. For all his deceptions and close conduct, Sharon would not have made full-scale war tolerable to a cabinet and opposition with eyes and ears if the possibility of a brilliant military-political coup had not been furtively acknowledged. If Sharon had very great interim powers, he also had total liability. He would have had the glory; as his very own self-nominated scapegoat, he did get the blame. 'Arik's war' his soldiers called it, and Arik's war would demonstrate how a string of victories may constitute a disaster.

The selection of the Maronites, in the person of the leader of one Maronite faction, as allies required a Maronite command of Lebanon to be sustainable. It required the majority Sunni Muslims and also the Shia Muslims, mostly living in south Lebanon not too distant from the Israeli border, to submit. It also involved graceful acceptance by the Druse, a heretical Muslim minority of only 6 per cent but militarily the most competent of all the Lebanese, whose mountain heartland was disputed with the Maronites. Machiavelli listed the dukes, marquises and city fathers who came running to King Louis's winning side when he was winning. But they didn't stay. There was nothing about the Maronites to keep other Lebanese on their side once the thrust of easy victory stopped. Historically, the Maronites had bossed the Sunnites, ignored the Shiites and engaged in a land feud with the Druse. The Maronites them-selves were united only by victory and by the readiness of Gemayel to kill his Christian rivals (see chapter 5). All the Maronites hated the Palestinians, but they were not available for fighting them. Israel was forced to act entirely on her own, without allies – an acute embarrassment in terms of interna-tional legality and respectability, factors a little more burden-some than in Machiavelli's time. But Israel categorically did not have the numbers or the means to control the entire state.

Machiavelli recommends that anyone who wishes to make himself secure should destroy the old leadership. Ironically, the Israelis were trying to shore up just such an old leadership to be their ally, only to have destruction wrought upon it by the Syrians and by the Maronites themselves. The Maronites, by contrast, had followed Machiavelli's orthodoxy. Bashir Gemayel killed Tony Franjieh and his family and had conducted a small massacre of briefly surprised troops serving Danny Chamoun. Bashir's own military followers, when they would set about the massacres of Palestinians at the Sabra and Shatilla, after his death, kept up the killing tradition, though more in unreasoning rage and natural barbarism. For the Syrians, targeting their key enemy in one room, would have killed Bashir Gemayel with a bomb. The Maronites were a frail basis for intervention at the best of times; with leaders eliminated, they began to define themselves as an old foundation being destroyed. All of Sharon's purposes for Israel in the Lebanon would be confounded, and all of Syria's perfectly served by this development.

The roots of the adventure, the very beginnings of folly, owed much to a visit from Alexander Haig. Schiff and Ya'ari, the excellent Israeli historians of these events, remark that his evident hostility to Syria as a Soviet connection instructed the extremist element within the Israeli leadership as to what they could do. 'By the time the Secretary left Israel, there was no doubt in many minds that with a man of Haig's bent running the State Department, Israel could definitely allow itself to adopt a militant posture *vis-à-vis* Damascus.' They record Begin as saying, after a closed, unminuted meeting with Haig, 'Ben-Gurion used to say that if you are pursuing a policy that may lead to war, it's vital to have a great power behind you.' Given America's record in sustaining Israel in conquest and repression, those words form into ice.

The war into which Israel was about to be drawn, with a great power stumbling about in the background, was never acknowledged as a war. Sharon had swaggered verbally; and in conversations with the American diplomats Philip Habib and William Brown he had in 1981 spoken of invasion, of eliminating the Palestine Liberation Organization from the Lebanon. He described to them a war (not altogether the war he was eventually to fight) in which Palestinians would be driven out of their encampments in Sidon and Damour. (This was closer to his fall-back plan of lesser aggression called, of course, 'Little Pines'.) About invading the Bekaa Valley or Beirut he did not speak. But through its appalled representatives, who reproached Sharon with his notion of the century he was living in, Washington knew of the general's broad inclinations. Basically Sharon would argue that Israel was threatened by Palestinian terrorism and beyond that by the Soviet Union, at this time still a player in the world, through her ally Syria.

He could not persuade Washington or the Israeli cabinet that there should be just such a war, candidly taken up for these purposes. But he could win broad empathy from Alexander Haig so that specific and categorical warnings-off did not come from the Americans. Begin, a furtive, moralistic ex-terrorist, was what in Ireland is known in the context of IRA crimes as 'a sneaking regarder' (as in 'I have a sneaking regard for the boys') – one wonderfully willing to acquiesce in acts which he had never authorized. The Israeli cabinet contained critics and opponents, notably the Communications Minister, another professional military man, Mordechai Zippori, but it was curiously passive, wanting neither to take the blame nor to miss out on any success. Indeed it resembled the lady in Vanbrugh's *Relapse* who, when sexually assailed, cries out for help under her breath.

But this was rape by increments as it was a putsch in slow motion. Sharon had made his contacts and preparations with the Gemayel gang over months. They were, as spelt out in chapter 5, to be his fighting allies when the struggle with the PLO took place. They were also to be his local cover in order that the mantle of some native interest should cover the too-blatant presence of the Israeli army or IDF. Ultimately they were to be his surrogates, his creatures or, in American, his 'good guys' as masters of the Lebanon accommodating to Israel. General Sharon had so many things organized, right down to the Soviet-friendly Syrians who were to be his decoy bogies. All he lacked was a pretext.

The spuriousness of formal occasions of war is illustrated by the conversation which Schiff and Ya'ari were able to report (villainous candour after the event being a redeeming feature of

Middle East politics), between Bashir Gemayel and Abu Zaim, head of intelligence to the Palestine Liberation Organization. According to this account, Gemayel gave the PLO the option of vacating the Damour district which they controlled and said that if they did not, 'You are undoubtedly acquainted with the scenario by which an Israeli baby is killed by a bomb in Acre, and Begin, after paying a condolence call on the parents, orders Sharon to invade Lebanon the next day.'

Yasser Arafat, when told, declined the invitation to treat. He had never been able to take Gemayel seriously – a reverse of Sharon's judgement in not only taking him seriously but believing him. War in any case came very quickly, by the medium not of a murdered baby but of a half-murdered ambassador. Shlomo Argov was shot and badly wounded outside the Dorchester Hotel in London. It would make no difference to Menachem Begin, or to the state of alarm and preparedness which Sharon had been building up in Israel, that the assassination attempt was in every particular an enterprise of Abu Nidal's organization. General Rafael Eitan, Sharon's rival and a man no more engaging, expressed himself in an old-fashioned Yiddish way: 'Abu Nidal, Abu Schmidal, we have to strike at the PLO.' Begin, not a man for nuance (or evidence), remarked, 'They're all PLO.' Thus, notwithstanding the facts that Yasser Arafat was known to Abu Nidal as 'the Jewess's son' and that Abu Nidal had sought to murder Arafat and had been ceremoniously sentenced to death by the PLO, facts could be allowed to blur and the occasion for the longed-for incursion was piously taken up.

The question at issue in cabinet was how far that incursion might go. Since it was supposed to be retributive and to clear the proximate pockets of PLO presence near the border, all discussion centred upon clearing PLO artillery so that the Jewish settlements (of which the United Nations and, officially, the United States disapproved) were out of its range. The distance involved was 40 kilometres. As Schiff and Ya'ari put it in Italic type: '*The only issue discussed at the Saturday night conclave was the need to push back the terrorist artillery.*' The operation even had a title, one which deserves to resonate: Operation Peace for Galilee.

Even so, doubt was expressed: The Minister for Communications, Mordechai Zippori, who suspected Sharon of seeking a full-scale war including a fight with the Syrians, spoke out. He had solid objections to any deal with the Phalange. The Phalange had their own interests into which Israel could be drawn; they had a conflict with the Syrians, so that any combination with the Phalange heightened the risk of having to fight Syria. Immediately, as a professional soldier himself, he questioned the distance airily agreed to. For a soldier a measured distance of 40 kilometres didn't mean very much. Armies don't count milestones and stop. He wanted an exact venue for the halt, otherwise they risked conflict with Syria. 'I have said that we will not attack the Syrians,' said Begin. 'It doesn't matter what we decide,' answered Zippori. 'The moves described here will bring us into contact with the Syrians.'

Sharon added his own gloss when the name 'Beirut' was mentioned. He said sharply, 'Beirut is outside the picture. Operation Peace for Galilee is designed not to capture Beirut but to drive the PLO's rockets and artillery out of the range of our settlements. We're talking a range of 40 kilometres. That's what the cabinet has authorized.' There was, in response to another question from Zippori, an estimate by Sharon of the time likely to be involved. 'I suggest we view it in terms of twenty-four hours. Up to the 40 kilometre point, however, things will be over before that.'

It proved to be not so; not so in almost every particular. The object was not just the clearing of 40 kilometres, but also the destruction of the PLO's northern forces. The only way to achieve that second object was to get behind the Palestinians, then take the Beirut–Damascus road and attack them in the rear. This was good soldiering; it wasn't 40 kilometres or twenty-four hours, but it delighted Menachem Begin who, at the next cabinet meeting, kept making circular gestures with his arms to describe the victorious sweep of his forces. By such a move – through the Shouf mountains and then east – the PLO would be encircled and obliged to choose between a fight or humiliating withdrawal from the Lebanon. It was supposed to be so compelling and crushing a manoeuvre that the Syrians would fall back in awe at it. 'A tactic worthy of Hannibal,' said the prime minister. As the Syrians were, by common consent, the most competent and tough of all Israel's putative opponents, this didn't seem the height of wisdom.

Nevertheless it got the cabinet out of the 40-kilometre bind even though the American President, Reagan, had just been given specific assurances that this was the furthest Israel would go. And as Sharon in a moment of elation conceded to uneasy military colleagues, there were Syrian surface-to-air missiles, with a brigade attached, blocking the route of that swoop; naturally they were to be removed – 'Everyone knew that.'

It is commonly the way of war and its requirements to change the ground upon which politics thought it had been standing. But the speed with which the Israeli cabinet was required to adjust from a 40-kilometre maximum to a big leap north beyond that, from no conflict with the Syrians to an invitation to Syria to stand or fly, would have put pressure upon the usual combination of docility, self-deception, humbug and awe of any government. Without Begin's senile duplicity, Sharon would never have got away with it. And even Begin, doting godfather of the adventure, had not been told of the requirement to take out the Syrian batteries. The 'everyone' of 'Everyone knows that' did not include the Prime Minister. He was given a military outline that omitted that essential. So armed and much elated, the Prime Minister, with twenty-four hours elapsed and the Americans knocking at his door demanding a cease-fire, offered his soldiers an extension of thirty-six hours for the short and splendid war he sincerely expected.

The reality would soon be expressed by General Sharon. 'The best solution I can see will be to move deeper into Lebanon,' he said before asking his commanders to speed up their advance on the Beirut–Damascus highway. 'We have to build up a context because we know that tomorrow we will take on the Syrians.' The general's regard for the truth in speaking to the cabinet, if expressed in a company report, would have entailed a custodial sentence. His commanders had hit problems of the kind which advances do hit and the war was going to take a little longer than the measure of hours promised, especially as the army got itself into its own militarized traffic jam. But such things happen and can be shrugged at by perfectly honest soldiers making fallible estimates. Where Sharon differed from the honest soldiers was that he wanted several wars: against the Syrians, against the PLO (beyond mere clearance of their southern artillery) – and, as Schiff and Ya'ari observe, he wanted them now. His demands for the capture of Jezzin, combined with the advance of General Menachem Einan upon the highway, were making conflict with Syria probable – a conflict for which he had exactly no mandate. But the key factor was the Syrian missiles which stood in the Bekaa Valley and which could be used against Israeli troops advancing on Ein Zehalta in the Shouf.

At this part of the front, another advance, that of General Avigdor Ben-Gal eastwards towards the Bekaa Valley, aroused doubts among Sharon's own senior officers. 'That', said Major-General Yekutiel Adam, 'means a war with the Syrians.' Didn't it contradict limits set by the cabinet? Major-General Mosha Levi objected that the army was not operationally ready for an assault on the Bekaa. Innocently Sharon proclaimed that he wasn't restricted from pursuing terrorists beyond the 40 kilometres, that if the Syrians were seeking a war, he couldn't help it and, most mendacious of all, that everything he did 'was anchored in the cabinet decisions'.

In a Pickwickian sense he was right, for when cabinet

reconvened on 9 June, though Zippori and another minister, Yosef Burg, demurred and asked questions about the 40-kilometre limit and the risk of bringing the Syrians into the war, Sharon gained an extension of his authority. To do so he changed tack and talked about the risk to Israeli troops in the Shouf if the Bekaa Valley missiles were not knocked out. The fact that Syria, an interested party in the Lebanon, had used her strong hand very lightly so far, skirmishing with helicopters but coming nowhere near all-out war, did not weigh as it should have done. The cabinet was blackmailed into acquiescence by the magic words 'our boys', having already let 'our boys' be sent where they had never meant to send them. By nibbling and pleading, by running extra unauthorized risks and demanding additional acts of war to cover those risks, Sharon made his salami war.

What followed was a successful operation in the military sense; twenty-nine Syrian planes were shot down, the missiles were destroyed, and a high proportion of carefully trained pilots were killed or otherwise put out of action. It might have been a brilliant victory won by disregard of the rules, as credited by history to Nelson. But we are describing what Machiavelli called a 'composite principality', composite in terms not only of the quarrelling groups that made up the Lebanon, but also of the powers that had an interest there, notably the Soviet Union and the United States. For all the hectic in Haig's blood for half-hours on end, the Americans emphatically did not want an Israeli–Syrian war which, having started as a minor clearance of Palestinians, could itself turn into something much larger, a conflict of patrons. Even Haig began to worry.

President Reagan, with the influence of his cooler, more far-sighted Defense Secretary Caspar Weinberger evident in his actions, ordered the Israelis to go back to their 40-kilometre limit. He did so in the knowledge that the foreseeable humiliation of her air power drove Syria back on to the Soviets and that the Soviets might feel compelled to redress the balance, perhaps even with their own pilots. The war, once rolling, rolled as Sharon wanted it to roll with a series of rather obvious deceits. The man who had told his cabinet colleagues that Beirut was off the agenda agreed a little later in the campaign to rendezvous with Phalange troops in Ba'abda. Ba'abda, a district which contains the presidential palace, is within the city boundaries of Beirut. Thus did Operation Peace for Galilee consummate itself as Operation Big Pines.

The battle itself had not been particularly easy. It had been won much as Britain would expect to win a war against the Republic of Ireland. The problem, exactly on that analogy, would be what on earth to do with such a useless victory and how to stand still in the territory taken. And the Syrians, like the Irish on most occasions, had put up a fight. Their air power might have been smashed, but on the ground they had fought hard and in their emplacements in the hills around and above Beirut they stayed put. Given unlimited time, they might have been cleared out; but there was a limit to American licence to Israel for operations on other people's soil, and people able to stop Sharon as the Israeli cabinet did not, stopped him. The Lebanon is not Syria's country as Ireland is that of the Irish, but then nor is it the country of the Israelis or the Americans; and having been neighbour and former suzerain, the Syrians have bossed it longer across history and will probably boss it longer in the future. The impossibilities which were now materializing had been foreseen and warned against by the chief of staff General Yehoshua Saguy, a man who was usually right but never got his own way. 'Whoever speaks about clearing out a 40-kilometre zone,' he had warned, 'is going to come to blows with the Syrians.' He also pointed out that the Soviets had promised men and *matériel* to Syria if she came under heavy pressure, that they would keep their word and that the Americans would (rightly) then blame Israel for running them into a fix. As for the Christians, Saguy had said, not foreseeing the death of Bashir, they wouldn't deliver on the battlefield nor would they stick with Israel which had come into their country. Further, they would want sovereignty over all Lebanon questioning or denouncing the influences Israel had enjoyed before the war, the links with Major Haddad's Christian militia and with the Shiites in the south.

It was the misfortune of a distinctly philistine military politician like Sharon to defy history only to find that bunk fights back; that history, like grass, grows over the heads of conquerors. If there had been no outrageous crime committed after the fall of Beirut, Sharon would almost certainly have still been frustrated. The 'marquis of Mantua' and the 'republic of Genoa' and the string of petty Italian nabobs listed by Machiavelli had bowed before King Louis in the second decade of the sixteenth century. So did the Shiites, the Druse and the several factions of the macaronic Christianity of the region defer to Ariel Sharon with the low, grovelling swoop of an Osric at the moment of his triumph. But as Saguy had patiently explained, they all looked confidently to a future in which, following the *coutume du pays*, they would once again pursue their ends and their enemies. And yet even these avid reverters to type could not have predicted the speed with which events occurred and caused General Sharon, in an American phrase, to come unglued. There *was* an outrageous crime and it was provoked by a more understandable, not particularly tragic killing.

The death of Bashir Gemayel is described in chapter 5. It came (on 14 September) at the end of a period in which he had exploited a war in which neither he nor his Phalange troops had fought, but which had left him the favoured client of the victorious invader, a status enjoyed for several years after 1940 by a number of European politicians, either Nazi-inclined or simply opportunistic. Laval, Quisling, Pavelic, Tiso, Nedic and their like were the role models, and the best parallel would be with the unbelieving schemer Laval, a man of similar beautiful, unflawed duplicity. Bashir, like Laval, now organized his own victory, in this case, through the collegiate election now due (this train was running on time) for the presidency of the Lebanon. With only the forms of reluctance, he was placed in the presidential palace. If he had been granted long residence there, he might perhaps have obliged General Sharon who had so obliged him, though we know Machiavelli's opinion on that subject. His interests did indeed lie with sustained resistance to the Syrians, enemies so animated that they were about to kill him. Equally, he could have seen a future for himself as a client through Israel of the Americans. He was, God knows, the type: 'A bastard but one of our bastards' (though he would have been his own bastard).

But speculation goes nowhere and neither did Bashir. The Syrians killed him. They might not be able to stop Ben-Gal's tanks, but they had a man in the innermost circles of the Phalange, a family connection almost. Habib Shartouni's cousin was an aide-de-camp of Pierre Gemayel. Such a man could enter and leave armed and castellated headquarters without troubling the concierge. And like Lorenzaccio★ to Alessandro de' Medici, Shartouni came.

The death of Bashir brought in his brother Amin who was moderately incompetent, not a proper party to the understandings which Sharon and Bashir had constructed and unable to prevent the quarrelling components of the Lebanon reverting to autonomous action at astonishing speed. But first something was to happen which echoed round the world. The Phalange troops (so little like the Israeli army which, even when pointed at illegality by a man like Sharon, was scrupulous about the laws of war) were at heart not soldiers, but rather tribesmen with a

★ Lorenzaccio (wicked Lorenzo) de' Medici, minor cousin of the head of the family and ruler of Florence, Alessandro de' Medici, ingratiated himself by charm, devotion and shared dissipations into a position of unexampled trust, and then invited Alessandro to dismiss all his servants for the night so that he might enjoy a citizen's wife that Lorenzaccio would bring to his bed. On his arrival, this dear cousin stabbed Alessandro to death and made good his escape, the subject of drama or fiction by Alfred de Musset and others.

gloss of gangsterdom. The death of Bashir pointed their strongest spirits at the Palestinians nearest to hand and also least able to defend themselves – those in the Sabra and Shatilla camps. The spirit of what happened is best described in the words of one of them, Jesse Soker, to an Israeli journalist, 'It's time you learned how to use a knife. But no rape of girls under twelve.' Another comment from a man reproached with the killing of women was that 'women bore children and give birth to terrorists'.

What matters is that on 16 and 17 September 1982 Phalangist Lebanese set about the murder of six to seven hundred unarmed people, including a number of women and children. The attitude of Israeli commanders during this crime was, to put it mildly, lax, uninquiring and un-urgent; in one judgement it was so naïve as not to be naïve at all.

Ironically for us, the rules of Machiavelli's sixteenth century, though not often time-altered, are affected by the vulgar emotions of the mass of people. Had mercenaries in the service of Florence murdered Pisans, it is hard to see the weavers of Florence much caring, and if they had, they would not have been taken note of. Disgust among the Israeli population and in the press, the feeling that Israel by furtive omission had been dragged into the dirty ways of the Lebanese, was the compelling reason for the train of events, including a commission under Chief Justice Kahan, which led to a withdrawal by degrees. Not that Justice Kahan's earnest attempt to set a full share of blame on Israeli commanders for their lethal passivity meant much in the rest of the Middle East. Palestinian propaganda fascinatingly absolved the literally red-handed Phalange and inculpated Saad Haddad, in his way the most honest man in the Lebanon and Israel's candid ally, and the Israeli troops themselves. Truth in the Middle East is not even a casualty; it is born dead.

As Israel rolled back, for a variety of reasons, Syria, knocked about in the war but intact and in the Lebanon, gradually began to emerge as boss dog. Attempts were made by the Americans to encompass their expulsion by holding out to the Palestinians that carrot's ghost, 'a solution for Palestine'. But the Syrians had not murdered Bashir in order to take orders from President Reagan's proxy, and they cooked up retributive trouble for Yasser Arafat in his own ranks for even talking to the Americans. More importantly, they stirred up the Druse, easily the most effective soldiers of all the native Lebanese, by backing their wish for an independent canton in the Shouf. The Druse, good for a killing any day, set about massacring Maronites, laying waste sixty villages and killing a thousand people.

A war between tribes is inexplicable to invaders and gives rise at home to calls that 'This is not *our* war' and 'Why not bring the boys back?' A war waged successfully against the head of state's tribe succinctly defines the extent of his writ. Amin's bluff was called almost before it was uttered. What was to follow is called the civil war in the Lebanon. It dragged on across the best part of a decade, turning murder into a chore, slashing the face and body of a handsome city. The objectives of General Sharon, for which he had finagled and blustered his way through cabinet, were either unaccomplished or undone. And to Wellington's melancholy sights of a battle lost and a battle won was added a third, yet more melancholy, of a battle neither lost nor won amid the wilderness which its waging had created. What Machiavelli uneasily concedes about the King of France in northern Italy has been proved true in the Lebanon. In this fashion a man may indeed cut a temporary figure, but without a settled ferocity and a clear undertaking of naked conquest with all its costs, he will not stay long.

CHAPTER THREE

The Overzealous Lieutenant: Mrs Thatcher ignores Machiavelli and cherishes three of them

(*The Prince* VII)

The notion of the over-zealous lieutenant is among the most fascinating in Machiavelli's text. It exemplifies better than anything else in the book the breathtaking coolness of Machiavelli's cynicism and yet is not at all forced or theatrical. Unforgivably, amid the refinements and civilities of official diplomacy, this truth stands at the centre of political psychology, of the way men exploit one another.

In the war between Iran and Iraq, the most zealous Iranian troops, men burning for martyrdom in an Islamic cause, were encouraged to lead the way across minefields, achieving in death all the delectations of the Muslim heaven and clearing a steady path on earth for their comrades. In the same spirit, Viking commanders employed at the front of battle, people whom they called 'berserkers' (literally 'shirt-only', in other words they had no armour or coat of mail to protect themselves by reason of being too mad). It survives in our word 'berserk', meaning violently crazy, and in its own time applied to those psychopathic personalities thought most fearful to the enemy and most readily dispensable.

True zeal in a cause does not make for charm and clubbability. But the truly zealous can be relied upon to do things which sensible, middling men pull back from. So it was with Stalin's NKVD henchmen, especially Yezhov, the purest ray serene of belief, less so with Hitler's Captain Röhm. For in his coarse, rough way, the head of the Sturmabteilung was a good deal saner and less homicidal than Hitler. Remirro de Orco (otherwise de Lorqua), murdered by Cesare Borgia, served both to dissociate that leader from excesses which had proved counter-productive and to give economical proof of his own quiet menace.

The basic idea is also charmingly simple. Hire dispensable men to do what you should not be seen doing, then if that act proves too intolerable, kill the dispensable men. The case can, however, also be proved by inversion. Do something controversial your-self, fail to off-load the blame on to lieutenants positively slavering for that sort of terminal glory and observe the opprobrium falling with pigeon-precision on your own head.

This proved exactly the case with Margaret Thatcher and the poll tax. Mrs Thatcher could be, on occasion, extremely circumspect and slow to take action and she could indeed make vigorous use of scapegoats. She delayed conflict with the powerful National Union of Mineworkers in 1981 when coal stocks were low (reserving that pleasure for 1984 when they were high). The union in that earlier year extracted excellent and uneconomic advantages from their action, with Mrs Thatcher foremost in retreat. Her Secretary of State for Energy, David Howell, who was, as it were, doing no more than standing about within reach of fate, was dispatched, making an end of the start of a promising career. It was a happier fate than that of Messer Remirro. Instead of being cut into two pieces for public display, Howell lingered as a lugubrious and expert presence on the back-benches, permitted not only to live, take up splendid business appointments in the Conservative ministerial manner, but in due course to become Chairman of the Foreign Affairs Committee, which involves several instructive trips abroad at the public expense annually, and also guarantees regular appearance on television as a respected public figure. We kill very much more nicely in England.

Mrs Thatcher acted as briskly in the case of the legislation to abolish the Greater London Council, enacted during the parliamentary session of 1984–5. Being bad-tempered and vindictive nonsense, it had failed to pass the House of Lords and had brought humiliation upon the government – almost, presumptuously, upon the Prime Minister. The cabinet member in charge, if that is quite the word, was Patrick Jenkin, not a prepossessing figure. His high, pained voice, always half-raised in ineffective protest at the unfairness of hostile observation and at things generally, almost cried out for real unfairness to be tried on him. It was.

As it happens, there was no need to abolish the GLC, guilty only, under the elegant leadership of Kenneth Livingstone, of cheeking Mrs Thatcher and contributing to the gaiety of nations. But anyone employing Patrick Jenkin would feel the urge to use him for a sacrificial offering, burnt or otherwise. His entire manner and style suggests Holman Hunt's picture, *The Scapegoat*. Sure enough, after their Lordships had overturned the bill, though Jenkin was kept on the interim strength as Environment Secretary, the work of repiloting the legislation was vested in a deputy, the looming and ascending Kenneth Baker, also a noted and enthusiastic henchman but one who enjoyed his work. And once the law was through, Jenkin made his way to the mild martyrdom of English politics, one subsequently crowned with some irony by strawberry leaves in that very House of Lords that had been his downfall; rather like hanging an architect from his own cross-beams.

But Mrs Thatcher, despite her grasp of other people's responsibility for her actions, despite the grim service of Bernard Ingham, a henchman's henchman who would detail a loyal colleague's unfitness for continued office, or indeed life, to representatives of the press before anyone told the loyal colleague, finally herself succumbed to zeal.

Local government finance, a dull paper in any university politics course, one taken only by people with a touch of tedium or serious ambition, had been a tribulation for some time. The rates system, immemorially rooted, but really important only since high-Victorian reform began, contained inequities, since as a tax through property, it did not need to reflect wealth accurately. It tended, and this was important to Mrs Thatcher, to be mildly unfair to the inheriting middle class. Much was made of the little old lady in the large house left to her by her husband, but living on a modest capital or pension. One can only say that any little old lady living in a large house during the champagne and marijuana housing market of middle-period Margaret Thatcher need have done only one thing: sell it for a grotesque, untaxed capital gain before going to live in a smaller house and pay much less in rates. To say this, however, is to be tiresomely rational.

Margaret Thatcher had two overriding obsessions (she had half a dozen others, but they need not trouble us here): deep emotional attachment to her own residential middle class, from the lower to the upper end of which she had risen on crampons, and loathing to the point of mania for local government. This did not at all exclude Conservative local government, which was not overly in love with her itself. The rates were rough and ready but they worked. That is, they were grumbled against and paid, which to a supporter of the market should be the only test. They raised the money, which was what concerned the Treasury. Those to whom they were at all unfair did not organize nationwide riot, refuse to pay or preoccupy politics for three years continuously. The simple glory of leaving moderately well alone had much to be said for it. But if the overrating of little old ladies truly troubled Mrs Thatcher – and there already existed rebates – those rebates could have been increased or speeded up for half of one per cent of the sum which would be spent once the Fifth Crusade of the Poll Tax was bloodily done.

Things went wrong partly because Mrs Thatcher's own reputation was being mocked. She had made a speech in 1976 which opponents liked to commemorate, calling for local government finance reform and specifically for an alternative to the rates. Little did these opponents realize quite how thoroughly they had poked a bear in the eye with a burnt stick each time that they remarked across 1983, 4, 5 and 6 how long it was taking the indomitable, the battling, the not-to-be-put-down Britannia-metal goddess to get round to doing anything about it.

Power had done many things to Mrs Thatcher, but it had done nothing for her judgement. With the winning of elections by the Conservatives, so it seemed in 1987, there was no end (it still seems, but not by her). Pride told her, backed by vanity, that what she wanted she could do, no matter who said it was impossible. The issue had been discussed long before, more than once indeed, but dull departments and ministerial committees had rejected alternatives to the rates with the cowardly objections that they were too dear, uncertain of efficient collection or politically explosive. All of this had been said in particular and in spades about the notion of a poll tax. It had, most grievously, been said by Michael Heseltine, twice. He was the relevant minister, he had seen the evidence and he is a shrewd, practical man.

He had also in 1986, under a blaze of television light, pre-empted any hint from Mr Ingham ('the sewer not the sewage' in John Biffen's phrase). He was gone in a diabolic magnesium blaze before that functionary had time to brief the press about his coming departure. Heseltine, often called 'Tarzan', maddened by Mrs Thatcher's disingenuous conduct in the matter of the Westland helicopters, had, as it were, jumped gallows and kicked her rump as he swung past to freedom. What Heseltine had been against, however dispassionately and without reference to the quarrel, could not be bad. Promoting the object of his scorn would be yet further proof of the mastery attributed to her by the less discerning newspapers.

The government of 1983–7, apart from beating the miners not as if they were wrong-headed and unwise but as if they were 'the enemy', and beating them in a way which left a whiff of Cossack in the nostrils, had not been very active or innovative. For all the noise, there was a large measure of holding-on and consolidation. The last part of the parliament had been darkly clouded by the Westland affair. There were charges of improper manipulation of confidential communications in order to influence a modest commissioning decision, manipulation then allegedly compounded by public frugality with truth. The truth, in accord with best British practice, never did come out, but the acts alleged were, in the eyes of those ill-disposed towards Mrs Thatcher, mad enough to be perfectly credible as hers.

In this mood of inertia garlanded with scandal, something positive was called for. This was looked to after the election victory – which, in the teeth of noise and incompetence, has always been the least of Conservative anxieties – in the form of a poll tax. (It is a measure of the vacuum nature of opposition at this time that Labour almost completely omitted to make an electoral issue of the poll tax. One shadow cabinet member, Jack Cunningham, pressed for it to be a major plank of the campaign, but was overruled, not least by extra-parliamentary advisers.) The underlying reason for thinking about the rates was the inability of government, for all its centralizing tendencies, to control the high spending of local authorities. As Nigel Lawson remarked to the Treasury Select Committee in 1985, Germany had a federal constitution with *Länder* which were genuinely accountable and France had a Napoleonic tradition of central authority served by prefects in the regions, while Britain fell sweetly between the two with central government hectoring, reproaching, threatening and paying. Local authorities were regularly outspending central government forecasts and making up the shortfall from higher rates. A convention of accommodation between government and town hall was breaking down. One might blame headline-catching left-wing authorities, one might look for wider causes. But the government's

[49]

concern would remain the same, to restrain local authority spending. Of course, the extra money might have come direct from government in the form of rate-support grant, with disastrous consequences for all plans on public expenditure. The irony of the poll tax was that it had precisely that effect; recourse upon recourse to the Treasury for more money was to extract huge covenanted sums. The object, accepted even by opponents of poll tax, of controlling local expenditure proved more risibly remote as that tax continued on its way, increased at every point by local councils happy to blame the government.

However, the immediate origins of this flagship of post-1987 governmental policy lay in local problems in Scotland. The rating system needs periodic revaluations everywhere, but in that unhappy country they must, by separate statute, occur every five years. The one scheduled for Scotland would have produced hideous consequences for uprated citizenry from Dumfries to Buckie. Major trouble from such citizens at the Scottish Tory conference helped to panic the Secretary of State, George Younger, and he had to be rescued by an interim subvention of £100 million from the Treasury (a happy thought to put to Scottish Nationalists). A poll tax looked (but only at first sight) a better alternative in Scotland and in a panic.

Mrs Thatcher turned at this point to a junior minister, William Waldegrave, deputy to the Environment Secretary, Patrick Jenkin, for further thought on alternatives to the rates. It was Waldegrave who, on the advice of Lord Rothschild, suggested a poll tax. According to Nigel Lawson this paper was taken up and accelerated by Mrs Thatcher herself at a Chequers meeting to which he 'foolishly, decided not to go'. Waldegrave argued for accountability by coupling a national business rate in place of non-domestic rates with a local residents' charge falling flatly, but with rebates for poorer people. Nevertheless, every-one would pay and the councils would be put on the line by their angry voters.

When the Chancellor found out what had been outlined at the Chequers meeting he drafted a memo quoted in his memoirs:

> The biggest gainers would be better-off households in high rateable value properties; the losers would be poorer households, particularly large ones . . . A pensioner couple in inner London could find themselves paying 22 per cent of their net income in poll tax, whereas a better off couple in the suburbs would pay only 1 per cent. We should be forced to give so many exemptions and concessions (inevitably to the benefit of high spending authorities in Inner London) that the flat rate poll tax would rapidly become a surrogate income tax . . . The problems of an old-style revaluation upheaval would of course be magnified many times during the period of transition from rates to poll tax. This is not simply a hideous political problem: local authorities would seize the opportunities to bump their spending and revenue and blame it all on the imposition by the government of an alien system of taxation . . . the proposal for a poll tax would be completely unworkable and politically catastrophic. A radical reform of the rating system seems a more attractive option.

Lawson, humanly enough, quotes his recorded opinions of May 1985 with some pleasure, but as he also observes: 'To my intense disappointment and some surprise, since the case seemed to me so clear, my objections received no support at all at the meeting of 20 May. Margaret invited Patrick Jenkin in to develop the Waldegrave proposals further . . .'

In fact responsibility passed almost at once to Kenneth Baker (Jenkin was now a posthumous lieutenant as a result of the affair of GLC and the House of Lords and was thus unavailable to be chopped in half again). Lawson is scornful of Baker, a mere presentationalist. But Baker, a proper politician however amenable to Mrs Thatcher, grasped something not apparent to zealots like the lady herself – that the only tolerable poll tax was one which happened slowly. His green paper *Paying for Local*

Government of January 1986 proposed freezing domestic rates so that their real input would decline with inflation. The Waldegrave residents' tax would start very low and rise to make up the shortfall. The greater the inflation or the council spending the more this poll tax would rise. It could then be blamed a little more plausibly, though one shouldn't have counted on it, on the council. Equally, interpolates Lawson, if it was going up absurdly and unpopularly, it could have had its clock stopped. The Baker proposals, known as 'dual running', were at least amenable to being modified after introduction, not an absolute state of affairs presented by way of revelation with a sprig of holly on top to an admiring nation. They also envisaged, even in their theoretical state, that the poll-tax would not become the solitary mechanism until the end of the century; the pain would fall in small increments.

Oddly, of all those involved in the poll-tax enterprise, Baker is the one who actually did get blamed, at least by way of mutter and whisper in the lobbies and print. The murmur was usually to the effect that he had moved on from his job at Environment to Education after sowing the seeds of calamity. However enjoyable to the opponents of Mr Baker, this is quite unfair; but in the context of Niccolò Machiavelli, unfairness is not a matter of concern.

At this point Mrs Thatcher won another election, something she could always get right, and in 1987 acquired the services of at least two more optional versions of Messer Remirro, lieutenants over-zealous to the point of self-evisceration. Michael Howard enters the scene as deputy to yet another Environment Secretary, Nicholas Ridley. Howard, now given the job of piloting the bill through, was a fast-promoted, ambitious and agreeable politician. He had entered ministerial ranks on the strength of a Commons speech defending the freezing of council-house sales revenue, a piece of central-command politics with no friends where there was understanding. Howard, a man of quick mind and forensic accomplishment, had cheerfully defended this indefensible and never looked back. Having gone nap on Thatcher, he stood ready on the up-curve of a ministerial career to defend the slaughter of the first-born.

Nicholas Ridley, the new post-election Secretary for the Environment, was a more formidable and more doctrinaire figure, but one with a taste for bitter conflict which would win him a choice of enemies. Later he would denounce the Germans. As key bankers within the European exchange-rate mechanism, they were running 'a German ramp' and up to no good. For the moment it was the poor. Lawson says that in earlier discussions, before the poll tax was too far advanced, Ridley had expressed doubts, even scruples, about its social fairness. Any hint of this disappears from his record as the responsible minister, and does so with the finality of doom. Arguments about the social equity of a tax falling without distinction upon the poor, the middling, the rich and all the people in between did not now impress him. He said as much to his local newspaper in Cirencester. 'Why should a duke pay more than a dustman?' he asked with defiant, courageous rhetoric much as Messer Remirro might have banged a citizen's head against a wall in Cesena. Ridley had both the stomach and the quarrelsome inclination to defend the poll tax for what it was: a tax so levied that the well-to-do, already blessed by large tax cuts, would pay a flat sum determined by numbers per household on equal terms with the very badly off and thus, proportionately to income, wealth and size of property, pay very much less. This was the truth of the tax, not something its advocates would wish to linger over.

This want of social finesse had been noted when the tax was last tried, in the reign of Richard II, when it had led to much unpleasantness. The poll tax was a species of fiscal nose-pulling which the rebarbative Nicholas Ridley, genuine aristocrat, genuine intellectual, inclined to confuse compassion with cant, was perfectly equipped to advocate. And in fact he was much more than its advocate. As has been made clear already, Nigel Lawson, supported by his successive chief secretaries, was at all stages against it; the rest of the cabinet was more passive than ardent; Mrs Thatcher herself was keen but her constitutional caution made her hesitate. One view, high in the cabinet, was that the lock of her mind was finally picked open by a memorandum sent by Ridley. By comparison, Messer Remirro was the merest hired hand. And if ever a man was perfectly primed to take the blame, not least because he deserved at least half of it, the man was Ridley.

Ironically though, Ridley – never unintelligent even when crashingly wrong – could see the means by which the poll tax would injure his own side. Accordingly in June 1987 he published figures to demonstrate that the poll-tax burden would be modest 'if it were not for local government overspending'. Since the tax had been imposed as a means to curb the hated local authorities, the fact of their being able both to spend *and* blame the government might have weighed against bringing it in.

No one could open himself up to blame with quite such panache as Ridley talking about the duke and the dustman. But Michael Howard, the first minister in charge of the enterprise *as legislation*, was aggressively confident about its wisdom, though, like all ministers, he avoided the actual words. The tax that dare not speak its name was referred to by Howard and all his colleagues at all times as the 'community charge', something which it seems Mrs Thatcher would angrily insist on at cabinet discussions. (Of all sauces to euphemism, 'community' is the most desolating; witness 'care in the community' for emptying the asylums on to the streets.)

Howard early became involved in dispute with the former Environment Secretary. Michael Heseltine, having stopped the proposal dead when in government, did not hesitate in exile to remind the public of the fact. He had twice advised the cabinet against introducing a poll tax 'and twice my advice was accepted. I have not yet seen any reason to change my mind and I shall listen to the reasons of ministers why they have changed theirs . . .' As much as Ridley, he took the point that Labour councils (and for that matter some Conservative ones) would, by spending more money, increase the size of the poll tax. But it would be no good, he said, to argue laboriously that they were then to blame. 'This', he memorably remarked, 'will be called a Tory tax.'

They were the government with the power, the credit and the blame. They had introduced the measure; if what happened next was nasty, all responsibility for it would fall on the Tories. This was advance warning by an expert. But Howard, with a barrister's bland confidence, announced that some reform of the rating system was inevitable and that all other options to the poll tax would produce worse results. But within a month of that remark, he and Ridley were attending an emergency meeting of back-bench Conservatives who were also grievously worried about the proposals. When the former prime minister, Edward Heath, spoke sharply on the subject, Howard expressed surprise that he should have 'attacked a proposal which has been a matter of consultation for eighteen months. One might almost suppose that the community charge burst unannounced into the Queen's speech and was an entirely new policy.' Given so long to think about it, and the policy being indeed a rather old, used and twice rejected one, he had fewer excuses for failure when, in a steadily mounting crescendo of public rejection, failure came. By September Howard was embarked on a series of speeches around the country to answer criticism of the tax. As they were made and he became more heavily identified, he was described by the journal *Agenda* as 'the Captain Nolan of the affair', an exquisite comparison. Captain Lewis Nolan, a brave Irish officer, adjutant to Lord Raglan during the Crimean War, carried the message to the Light Brigade that it should charge.

But Captain Nolan did not originate or even agree with the message he brought. According to Lawson again it was Howard who 'began an energetic lobbying campaign to persuade parliamentary colleagues that "dual running" was an abomination and that a clean switch from the rates to the poll tax was preferable'. He was acting in concert with Ridley who later observed, 'It never seemed to me right to have two taxes in operation at once, and the accountability advantages to the community charge would be completely obscured.'

They did not, however, confine themselves to opinion and campaign. They found a way to change policy completely and throw Baker's safeguards out of the window. The Conservative party conference, never democratic, had latterly become a rally and an act of worship. But its wishes could be given importance if the person in charge followed the whim of responding to views close to her own heart. The run of speakers from the floor at conference was, according to Lawson, contrived by Ridley and Howard to create pressure for an abrupt introduction. The speech best remembered was one fervently demanding 'the poll tax now' from Gerald Malone, a good chap normally, but on this occasion an over-zealous lance-corporal. Margaret Thatcher, so Ridley relates, whispered into his ear, 'We shall have to look into this again, Nick'. The cabinet committee was duly convened; Ridley announced to it his desire to be rid of dual running. Over Lawson's head, Ridley's wishes prevailed. The poll tax went forward in a telescoped, accelerated form to delight Labour councils running up bills and left-wing agitators starting marches and/or riots, while distressing both the Treasury, which now had to start a series of subventions to stop successive screams of pain, and poorer people who did the screaming. Chopping Ridley in half in Old Palace Yard would have been leniency.

The same article which had compared Howard to Captain Nolan had observed: 'Capped poll tax will enable councils to pass the buck for the resulting chaos to the Tory government, just as they do now with capped rates. A capped poll tax will be a Treasury tax in all but name' – exactly the point made earlier by Michael Heseltine. Howard was forced into arguments that are very easily taken apart. In a written reply in the Commons he claimed that 8.8 million households would be gainers from the poll tax and an equal number would be losers. The idea that it was acceptable for 'only' half the country's households to be on the losing side suggests an excessively arithmetical cast of mind.

Meanwhile another complication had set in, for which Nigel Lawson, acting for the best, must take responsibility. He had put up the readily accepted proposal that the poll tax should fall upon Scotland a year ahead of England and Wales. Malcolm Rifkind, who should have known better but was persecuted by Mrs Thatcher for lack of keenness, embraced the plan. Lawson's intention, of course, was to provoke the salutary warning that was delivered by ill-will at conference in Inverness and by the massed regiments of Scottish grievance. He looked for a remonstrance and the Tories got it, but Mrs Thatcher was no longer equipped to listen.

The fact that reflexively surly Scotland is more radical and left-wing than England, even in the outlook of its middle class, should have warned ministers that no worse place for a poll tax could be imagined. The process chosen and followed – a year of the tax in Scotland to get it bedded down, followed by enactment in England and Wales – was a piece of textbook ineptitude.

Scottish pride being the field of pits sown with spikes and land-mines that it is, Scotland was certain to take massive affront at having to provide a trial run. She did, responding immediately like a neurotic cheetah treated like a laboratory mouse. A revival of the often dormant, never extinct, nationalist cause was one result and about the last thing that Scottish Conservatives, down to their last 19 per cent of the vote, could have wanted. Furthermore, Scotland has a tradition of defiance of the central power, so that a campaign of non-payment, however strongly opposed by the Labour Party, would attract significant support and would directly influence the reaction a year later in more submissive England and Wales. In any case, all militant protest benefits from dithering. If you must be despotic, it is wisdom to be despotic in a swift, conclusive way, or very slowly and painlessly *à la* Baker. For Mrs Thatcher – who was after all only trying to demonstrate her decisive qualities – to display them by means of a dress rehearsal was an elementary tactical error.

In response to the growing anxiety, Sir George Young, a genuinely respected former minister, significantly also a future minister, proposed an amelioration of the poll tax, asking that it should be banded, with the payers taxed according to their means. Banding was a way out; however arbitrary at the margins, it would restore a rough social justice to payments. By accepting it, Howard, Ridley and Thatcher would have performed a retreat, what politics since Edward Heath's pull-back in 1971 has called a 'U-turn'. The Conservative government would have been mocked for a week, but would thereafter have been united and inoculated against street politics. The threat of non-payment would have been much reduced and the greater U-turn of dismantling the poll tax, which was eventually executed after the fall of the Prime Minister, avoided.

Such good sense was not to be contemplated. The whips were bidden to organize the defeat of the proposal when, at the instance of another Conservative, Michael Mates, it was put to the House. And despite mounting discontent in the country and anxiety in the party – expressed even by solid right-wingers such as Sir Rhodes Boyson, who knew a thing or two about local government and about the London suburbs – defeat it they did. The message came – from voters and rioters – 'The struggle continues'.

Not, however, for Michael Howard. Instead of being blamed for his leading part in a piece of consummate folly, he escaped to be given responsibility for another dubious measure, the privatization of water, which would bring in high profits and higher prices to the infinite satisfaction of quite small numbers of people. It was as if Messer Remirro had been told after his exploits in Cesena to go off and beat up Bologna.

The chalice passed to Michael Portillo, a whizz with technical details, and devoted to Mrs Thatcher in ways more appropriate to the Blessed Virgin Mary: clever on paper, vastly ambitious, but not sensible. His earliest ejaculations on the topic included the observation that 'it puts power into the hands of local people'. To these he added a phrase belonging in all good books of quotations, that the poll tax was an election-winner.

What actually unfolded, as legislation became law, was one of the great disasters of modern elective politics. The Department of the Environment had talked of a poll tax averaging £200 per head without any thought of subsidy or lifeboat. By 1990 the figure had become £400. This was blamed (by Ridley) on local authorities putting up staff numbers and bills and then blaming the government, something he understood after it had happened but unaccountably had not envisaged when promoting and accelerating the tax.

The poll tax would also be distinguished for non-collection, £2 billion, or ten per cent of expected revenue, falling short in year one. Yet still there was no prime ministerial flight from humiliation, nor was any act worthy of Cesare Borgia visited upon the culprits. Mrs Thatcher by late 1989 was a bit like Oscar Wilde not escaping on the boat-train. The culprits prospered: Howard was made a full cabinet minister, while Ridley was promoted to the Board of Trade where he might brood upon the wickedness of the Germans and the European Community. He was indeed eventually sacrificed, but only at his own hands and on the altar of his own prejudices after giving an eccentric interview, berating the Germans, to Nigel Lawson's journalist son Dominic.

His successor at Environment was Chris Patten, a different sort of politician, from the Tory left, who promptly obtained in

1989 the sum of £2.6 billion as extra local government grant, then a further £345 million, much less than he wanted, the same year.

Once the poll tax came on stream it inevitably produced massive discontents, including factitious far left-wing ones which, when setting the wrong sort of demonstrators against the wrong sort of policemen, produced riots in more than a dozen places. But this was nothing politically to the civil protest of non-demonstrators. Quite poor people, starting the year in a low-rated property in an inner city, suddenly acquired multiplied poll-tax bills. Quite poor authorities were hit, Conservative MPs grew insistent about their local griefs, and a succession of emergency measures were hurried forward to temper the effect. As such attempts were made to spread the cost around, they in turn infuriated people, not themselves necessarily wealthy, in wealthier towns who nevertheless found themselves paying more. So finally, after the fall of Margaret Thatcher, another £3 billion would have to be found by Michael Heseltine, Environment Secretary in the first Major government, by way of yet further support for local government. This in turn would be paid for by a 2.5 per cent increase in VAT.

If the consequences of the poll tax were calamitous for individuals and for Treasury calculations, they also afflicted the Conservative and Unionist Party. The malaise was reflected in opinion-poll figures putting the Conservatives close to third place and in the sort of by-election results – like the huge Tory defeat in the Ribble Valley constituency – that looked like misprints. When, in late autumn 1990, after a party conference in Bournemouth like the first two acts of a play with a death in the third, a by-election deprived them of Eastbourne, that Jerusalem of the middle classes, the Conservatives knew what to do and did it. The fall of Margaret Thatcher after eleven and a half years in power – unprecedentedly removed as unfit to govern, which in all conscience she had been for some time – was a light affair by sixteenth-century Florentine standards, but a matter of literal weeping to Portillo, grief to Ridley and regret to Howard.

It was also inexorable judgement on a mistake made in detail across five years from the first approaches and Waldegrave's paper, a mistake which could have been ended or mended half a dozen times. It was, above all, one for which those who had a share of the guilt – the egregiously silly Portillo, the insistently ideological Ridley or the optimistic Howard – could, in the high Machiavellian manner, have taken *all* the blame. The scenario is not difficult or bloody: '*Of course* the community charge is a splendid idea *in principle* but although Nick/Michael/Michael have done *wonderful* work and will go on giving every help in the House of Lords, I think that perhaps they care too much and that we must be a little less idealistic in what we try to do . . .'

Instead, Margaret Thatcher chose her own judgement against better advice and held tight to counsellors who, from political affinity, calculation or the fearful thrill she had made natural, wanted what she wanted. To those who were wrong in her way, Margaret Thatcher remained dimly loyal. Once pride and preoccupation had got the better of her, she constituted no threat to any lieutenant on her long path to self-destruction, having herself become the over-zealous captain.

CHAPTER FOUR

Those who come to power by crime: The rise and fall of Captain Röhm

(*The Prince* VIII)

Machiavelli chose for his exemplars of men rising by crime Agathocles the Sicilian and Oliverotto of Fermo: one from the classical age, the other an Italian contemporary. It was the sad folly of Oliverotto, having betrayed, double-crossed and killed his uncle and protector in the most exemplary fashion, to commit the elementary solecism of first opposing Cesare Borgia and then trusting him. The consequence of such innocence in attending the Renaissance equivalent of a party conference in the seaside resort of Senigallia, was, in company with other opponents of the Pope's son, to be handily garrotted by Spanish mercenaries sentimentally employing a folk method of dispatch.

A fair parallel with such historical heavies might well be Ernst Röhm, head of the Sturmabteil (SA) (the force of paramilitaries in brown uniforms who enforced on the street for Hitler before 1933), though he illustrates quite as well Machiavelli's doctrine of the unique dispensability of the over-zealous lieutenant. Röhm rose by crime to be sure, but he also reminds the student of one of Machiavelli's star victims, that same Messer Remirro Dorco, who made enemies in Central Italy by employing too much force. Dorco, like Captain Röhm, demonstrated the moderation of the man who killed him.

Röhm, though, also differed from most members of the Nazi party (NSDAP) by being coolly objective and often hostile towards Hitler. Unlike Hess, Goebbels or even the independently important Goering, he would call him not 'Mein Führer', but 'Adolf', a mistake never again made by anyone else. Although Röhm did indeed rise by crime – street violence of the most sustained and admired sort, the beating-up of citizens and street clashes with the private armies of other political parties, notably that of the Communists – he was better connected than Hitler: not an NCO but an officer, if not exactly a gentleman. As adjutant to the head of military intelligence in Munich immediately after the First World War, he had also been Hitler's patron. When Hitler was a corporal and freelance spy reporting on radical and Marxist movements within the army, it was Captain Röhm who directly commissioned him.

Even Hitler's involvement with the political party whose chrysalis he would take over, rename and transform was almost certainly a piece of routine work undertaken by the ex-corporal on behalf of Captain Röhm and Reichswehr Intelligence. The German Workers' Party, under a microscopically small-time leader, Anton Drexler, was investigated by agent Hitler and found to be whistle-clean in its patriotic sentiments. But according to the same source it was also 'the lowest form of political club life . . . without even a miserable rubber stamp', and it was subsequently devoured by the debating talents and personality of the seventh recorded member of its committee, a spy.

In the opaque period between the end of the First World War and the unsuccessful Munich putsch of 1923, Hitler was dependent upon Röhm for funds to sustain the new party and for contacts, otherwise unimaginable to a corporal (even one holding two classes of Iron Cross), with senior military officers. Röhm did not invent Hitler but he made him possible. Functioning at all times as his patron and channel to the official military, he represented the Austrian as the most apt of many people useful for patriotic but illegal undertakings. Before the war and without Röhm, Hitler had been an odd-job man and vagrant; after the war and with Röhm, he was a rising figure in serious (if extreme and provincial) politics. He had made the journey as a runner, a *Vertreuensmann* or trusty, a low-level, dependent informant who gave satisfaction.

Röhm himself was, by contrast, a natural *condottiere*, a soldier of fortune who would leave the German scene for several years, from 1925 to 1930, as a mercenary adviser in a South American war. But within Germany, his natural habitat was the Freikorps, the bands of paramilitaries with broadly nationalistic and military sympathies who roamed the country for several years after 1918, not quite legal and not quite not, in a period when civil government existed in form but not always in substance. The discharged troops of an army which had been limited by the rhapsodic folly of the Versailles treaty to 100,000 men were available in numbers altogether greater than that during a period of hyperinflation and extensive unemployment. They were only too willing to paraphrase the army, wear uniform, stage marches, do a little fighting and a little killing.

They also sporadically attempted to seize power, as in the Kapp putsch of 1920 and Hitler's own 1923 excursion in Munich. The experience of trying for power illegally and without the army convinced Hitler that he must on all occasions seek power legally and with the army. Ironically, Röhm, an altogether more regular soldier, took a more cavalier view of his superiors despite being essentially loyal to them in a way not appreciated as they applauded his death.

Until the murder in 1922 of the Foreign Minister, Walther Rathenau, most Freikorps activity was widely appreciated by the civilian population which was outraged at the docking of the army. Many of the public were also indifferent to the new liberal forms of government and fearful of a left-wing threat on the Soviet pattern. The left would, in reality, show itself altogether stronger in cabaret than revolution. Also, the alternative mechanism for keeping an army above treaty requirements would be to keep forces within the boundaries of the Soviet

Union with Soviet consent, something Germany would actually do in the twenties.

The approved status of the Freikorps in certain regions was illustrated by a comment of Ernst Pöhner, police president of Munich. A democratic politician called upon Pöhner to complain that political murder gangs existed in Bavaria. 'I know,' said Pöhner, 'but not enough of them.' Not everyone felt the same way. In resisting an early attempt at a putsch, a Communist mob in Chemnitz captured one Freikorps leader and putschist, the distinguished and supremely decorated fighter-pilot Rudolf Berthold, and strangled him with the ribbon of his *Pour le mérite* insignia.

The Freikorps were, like Röhm himself, a mercurial and uncertain force. Although fervent nationalists, and soldiers by choice, they were not necessarily and universally conservative. Many of the young soldiers shared with Ernst Röhm an active loathing of the rich, the inheriting and the privileged. Many minds were in a state of flux. The two young men, Kern and Fischer, who murdered Walther Rathenau, Foreign Minister, industrialist, social thinker and arguably the most intelligent and enlightened man in Germany, had heard him speak and been profoundly impressed with this advocate of social reconciliation. 'Rathenau is our hope,' wrote Lieutenant Erwin Kern, 'for he is dangerous . . . he is indeed the finest and ripest fruit of his age. I couldn't bear it if again something great were to arise out of the chaotic insane age in which we live . . . We are not fighting to make the nation happy but to force it to tread in the path of its destiny.' The murder was an act of Wagnerian mysticism, the sacrifice of a hero as act of purgation, spilt romanticism flowing as blood. It was completely at odds with the crystalline rationality of Machiavelli.

With young minds and violent spirits walking the earth, the phrase 'National Socialist' was not hypocritical however slyly chosen; it expressed something then very prevalent in Germany, a mixture of patriotism, militarism and non-revolutionary social reform based on social resentment – a sort of vicious moderation. And Ernst Röhm in 1934 stated that Hitler shared his contempt for the moneyed element. The statement was entirely correct and one of the reasons why Hitler had him murdered.

The Nazi Party required at all times to retain the flow of funds coming to it from the Bechsteins, Thyssens and other rich, unpopular people in business, and yet to keep up the spirits of disinherited, unprivileged young men willing to swagger and terrorize for it on the streets. It had also to retain the sympathies of a Reichswehr which by turns looked to it and down on it. With the army very much in mind, it had to balance legality with illegality. As an army man and an officer, Röhm was able to bring Hitler cash and access to highly placed and cautious friends – also, as a wholesale handler of military personnel, he was able to point soldiers in the direction of the Nazi Party.

As an army man, he wished in the mid-twenties that the Sturmabteilung (or Frontbann or Kampfbund as it was variously called), should serve the purposes of the army by being a hidden reserve of unofficial soldiers. Hitler required it to be absolutely subordinate to the party and to him. This was the difference which led, as interim peace and employment settled down in the mid-twenties, to Röhm's temporary withdrawal from Nazi activity and his departure to supervise a small war in another hemisphere.

When he came back in 1930 and in mid-crisis to provide the Nazis with an intimidatory force on the streets, Röhm was outstandingly successful; the figure put on the troops at his disposal was 400,000. He was certainly a beneficiary of raging unemployment, but his Brownshirts became models for the bare-knuckle right throughout Europe. The Freikorps had been a scatter of diverse, ill-coordinated groups under many commands, a sort of anarcho-militarism. Röhm commanded, loosely but as one force, the means to total power. He might have been seen by a fearful observer as the man capable of achieving government by seizing it, both before and after 30 January 1933. He was the man owed gratitude (and thus death) by Hitler who *was* such a fearful observer.

He was the commander of an army bigger than the army. He was also in increasing conflict with Hitler over both the role of his troops and policy. At heart Röhm was a radical, critical not only of the upper class and the rich who had been brought a secure if not altogether quiet life by Hitler's access to power, but of the too-conservative and privileged army with which he wished, on his own terms, to merge the SA. To that army he was, however, faithful after his fashion. In circumstances of mortal conflict, critical fidelity may be seen to be the worst of all combinations. If Röhm had not been critical, he would have caused no anxiety. If he had not been loyal he would have taken power. With textbook folly, he set out his views candidly and then took no action. To speak of 'a brown tide covering the grey rocks' – the SA wore brown and the Reichswehr grey – was not altogether wisdom.

Still less was it wise to accept Hitler's request that the SA be sent on leave for the month of June, 1934, a blunder that Röhm compounded by issuing this order for the day: 'If the enemies of the SA think that it will not return from leave, let them enjoy their illusions while they can. When the day comes these people will receive an adequate reply, in whichever form necessity dictates. The SA is, and will remain, the destiny of Germany.'

Provocative rhetoric without the employment of force is a fundamental error. The illusion was Röhm's, and when the day came (very quickly), he was invited by the enemies of the SA to shoot himself. His reply, good but hardly adequate to the situation, was 'Let Adolf do his own dirty work' – something no one seriously exercising political power has ever found necessary. He was shot instead at point-blank range by two SS officers, and the SA lost all connection with destiny.

It was desirable to destroy so strong-seeming a man because he was now so much more useful dead; it was possible because at all times his menace outran his will. Destroying him and his forces did more than remove a threat (aggressive, noisy and not politically ingenious, he was perhaps never that), it made it possible for his murderer to claim that a little killing now assured the nation's ease and quiet. Everything had been done in the name of safety and public security. Also of respectability; it happened that Röhm and many of the men around him were unapologetically homosexual, Röhm himself being of the passive, feminine sort.

Hitler shared none of the petty-bourgeois prejudices of Sir John Junor. The circle of young men, heroic or epicene, around the SA command had caused no adverse comment from a leader who prided himself on a Bohemian and artistic *savoir-faire*. But upon the Chancellor of Germany, appointed by conventional conservatives seeking someone to do their dirty work for them, a Chancellor whose electoral success had depended on the cheques of the Düsseldorf Herrenklub, Rotarian imperatives were more pressing. The preparation of a dossier on Röhm's sexual life had been commissioned from Diels, head of the Berlin Gestapo, well in advance of the decision to shoot him. His death would be the signal for further and detailed assassination. Like Stalin, Hitler regularly did solid business by proclaiming himself as the moderate in any conflict. This was reflected in the praise given to the Night of the Long Knives by a distinguished non-Nazi professor of law, Carl Schmitt, who in the *German Law Journal* of 1 August 1934 described the retrospectively legalized erasure of opponents as 'direct justice' and 'the highest law' of the new order. The title of Schmitt's piece was 'The Führer Protects the Law'.

Röhm may have risen by crime, but in the great perspective of the Third Reich it was petty crime; worse, it was noisy, oafish, theatrical crime of a sort deplorable from all angles of public relations. Killing him gave Hitler an opportunity of demonstrating to stupid people his abhorrence of excess, and to brighter people the cold-blooded facility for death which has always impressed in statesmen.

It was Röhm's tragedy that he functioned at all times as a bogy. Before 30 January 1933 Röhm and the SA usefully frightened democratic politicians and the voters, and they had more than the edge over gangs of the left. But with these enemies dispelled, the army in probationary amity with Hitler and Hitler formally elected Chancellor, the SA continued to inspire fear. Alarm had now spread to the new middle-class allies of the Chancellor, the business and financial communities and, most important of all, the army. In political terms, Röhm and the Sturmabteilung had become uneconomic. It was time, in the way of retail lines, for them to be discontinued, in that of coal-pits, to be closed, in that of armed men threatening other armed men, to be shot dead.

It was all done – the SA part of the Night of the Long Knives – in a manner astonishingly reminiscent of Cesare Borgia's conference at Senigallia. The SA were also to meet their leader to discuss differences at a conference. This one was to be at a hotel in Bad Wiessee on 30 June 1934. Hitler, in the manner of all successful putschists, arrived early, with troops. They seized the SA leadership literally from its beds and bundled them off to Munich where over three days the actual shooting took place. A decree declaring the acts of 30 June and 1 and 2 July to be legal as a defence of the state was authorized by the cabinet on 3 July.

The occasion was also used to kill Gregor Strasser, a Nazi of the left who commanded a faction, Edgar Jung, a Catholic academic who had written for the Catholic politician Franz von Papen a speech, critical of Hitler, which was greatly beyond Papen's small and furtive capacities, a couple of minor characters with knowledge of Hitler's private life, and Willi Schmid, music critic on the *Münchener Neuer Nachrichten*, shot in mistake for Willi Schmidt, a minor SA officer, also shot.

Captain Röhm had the misfortune to combine obligation from a dangerous man with inconvenience to him, to be free-spoken in circumstances demanding extremities of discretion, and to be an imaginable alternative to his leader. Of the men

[69]

around Hitler in his time of very great power, only Goering and Goebbels were of outstanding ability. The one was debilitated by drugs and lethargy, the other accepted and embraced subordination in a fashion gratifying to the head of any enterprise. Hitler did not, as a general rule, behave with great severity towards his associates, and after 30 June 1934 he had no need to.

Röhm would have been entirely happy and entirely safe had he been the military right hand of Mussolini. The Italian, in any case a vastly more tolerant and merciful man, would have discounted the 80 per cent of rhetoric in Röhm's mutterings as the operatic wind it was. Il Duce would then have been served until the end by a lieutenant frequently grumbling but in every way more trustworthy than those who at the Grand Fascist Council in 1943 would remove him from office.

The perfect symmetry of Hitler's actions on the Night of the Long Knives was to have ingratiated himself with the military command and the middle classes by killing the man who had introduced him to the middle classes and the military command. Furthermore, by shooting people who seemed likely to oppose him then for the instruction of people who might oppose him in the future, he discouraged that faintheartedness in adversity which was to betray Mussolini. He instilled into generals, bankers and other members of his party a fear so fervent and vital that when he fell, it would be by his own hand and those of invading armies brought across a continent and an ocean against him. Even so, in July 1944 he had been obliged to rerun the reel.

A man may indeed rise by crime only to fall much more spectacularly by greater crime, and all lieutenants stand instructed by the example of Ernst Röhm of their utility as scapegoats.

CHAPTER FIVE

Further and better *coming to power by crime*: The exploding star of Bashir Gemayel

(*The Prince* VIII)

The rise of Bashir Gemayel would have given great pleasure to Machiavelli, for whom the experience would have been rather like watching the achievements of a prize pupil. For if ever a man rose by crime, Bashir did; and in the annoying way of untidy events, he also exemplified in his dealings everything that Machiavelli ever said about the lame second place of that unfortunate virtue, gratitude. Bashir started with the basic equipment of a Renaissance prince, inheriting a place in the game, but ancient enmities and immediate rivals along with it. He was the younger son of Sheikh Pierre Gemayel, whom western newspapers would refer to as a prominent Lebanese politician, but whom Machiavelli would have recognized as a minor ruler and head of a tribe. They would also speak of Sheikh Pierre as a Christian leader. 'Christian' in the context of the Lebanon must be understood strictly as a group identity, remote from any imaginable moral or ethical standpoint. In any game of consequences played in the Lebanon, the word 'Christian' would most likely be followed by the word 'massacre'. Bashir Gemayel was so much of a Christian that he would have aroused professional admiration in that champion of the papacy, Cesare Borgia.

Power within the Lebanon was divided, and had been since the end of French suzerainty, by an apportionment of office between Christians (Maronites, country members of the Roman Catholic

Church) and Sunni Muslims on a 6:5 ratio. It was slightly more complicated than that, involving the sub-interests of Greek Orthodox, Shia Muslims and finally of Druse, followers of the Caliph Hakim, who made up 6 per cent of the population, most of them in the Shouf and adjacent mountain regions. It was also understood that the prime ministership would always be in the hands of a Sunni and the presidency in those of a Maronite.

The Maronite Christians were split among themselves along family lines in a sense theoretically intelligible to the Florentine Machiavelli, but more immediately so to someone from Naples of south of it. Actually, the division of power in the streets of Beirut would come, at the time of the civil war, to bear closest resemblance to the apportioning of Chicago in its great days. The principal Christian families were those of Franjieh, Chamoun and Gemayel. At the time of the Lebanese crisis in the mid-seventies, Suleiman Franjieh held the presidency, not that it did him much good as the weapons of the PLO assailed the air-raid shelter that was his headquarters. Camille Chamoun had taken great risks with the integrity of the Lebanon in 1958 by inviting an American force to intervene in his problems of the day, while Pierre Gemayel had expressed his family ambitions back in 1936 by starting a political party, the Phalange, in the very year that General Franco, ally of the Spanish Falange, made his Hitler- and Mussolini-aided pitch for power and precipitated the Spanish Civil War.

Naturally the Phalange had a militia, and Lebanese politics resembled those of southern Europe thirty years earlier, the street-arrangements of a Fascist Christian right against its enemies. But this is the age of public relations and, in a spirit of adaptability which would have charmed George Orwell, the Gemayel grouping's name would subsequently be changed to the 'Social Democratic Party'. The armed followers of Chamoun were known more succinctly as the Tigers. But the Gemayel heavies were integrated, long-established, better armed and more effective. The time would come when, in a dispute between

Christians, the Social Democrats would prove the merit of understatement by slaughtering the Tigers.

If the Lebanon was uneasily divided between two sorts of Christians and three kinds of Muslims plus the Palestine Liberation Organization which had entered the country in 1969, that country was also the anxious concern of many nations outside: at the very least, Israel, Syria and the United States. Such interest as Egypt had once had in the Lebanon, however, had been eloquently discounted in the words of Anwar es-Sadat speaking to the Israeli Prime Minister, Menachem Begin. He was describing Camille Chamoun, but it might have been any prominent Lebanese Christian: 'Let Chamoun be. He is a despicable human being. He was an agent of the British, the French, the Americans, the Syrians and now he's your man.'

The crisis which would give Bashir Gemayel his opportunity was the effective loss of Maronite supremacy in the Lebanon. The PLO, in alliance with the Druse, had challenged the Lebanese national army and won. Beirut was divided by barricades, Maronites in outlying villages had been slaughtered and the city of Zahle was surrounded. The Christian leaders might be despicable human beings, they might have brought most of their troubles on their own heads, but they were entitled to seek rescue and they did so by turning to one of the three patron onlooker states, Israel.*

Bashir Gemayel was part of the delegation sent for first tentative meetings with the Israelis in 1976. He cut a slight and foolish figure at that time. Insisting on wearing a mask for his shipboard meeting off the Lebanese resort of Junieh, he gave the Israeli intelligence officers to whom he spoke the impression that they were dealing with a child. He and his elder brother, Amin, despite (or perhaps because) of American education and qualification as lawyers, lacked authority. The acute shyness of

* For details of the Israeli invasion of the Lebanon, see chapter 2.

Bashir was noted and the view was expressed that he might at any time burst into tears.

The Israelis were to be far more impressed by another spokesman that they met some time later, namely Danny Chamoun, younger son of Camille. Chamoun was candid about not being a soldier himself, but was uncomplicatedly ready for action and alliance, plainly asking for arms and help with which to fight the Palestinians. He also had a certain style, a touch of social assurance which went down well. Less well received was the evidence of the Maronite war effort shown the same day during a follow-up meeting at the villa of Camille Chamoun himself, the 'despicable human being'. Young women, introduced by the old godfather as Christian militia, were asked by an Israeli what they had accomplished. In reply they unpacked two plastic bags, one containing fingers, the other ear-lobes, all allegedly cut, one per body, from Palestinians.

Israeli disgust did not stop the diplomatic effort, and lines were established to both the Chamouns and the Gemayels as controllers of forces hostile to the PLO; an enemy's squabbling enemies who should be encouraged to co-ordinate their command and efforts. Despite contact, no such link was established with the Franjieh family because, taking a different view of their own and possibly the Lebanon's interests, the Franjiehs preferred Syria as patron nation. Tony Franjieh, also a member of the cabinet (a notably corrupt Minister of Posts) and a prominent entrepreneur in the wholesale hashish market, controlled the family's military forces. He attended one social meeting with the Israeli representatives, talked affably but indicated firm disinclination for any deal between his grouping and the Israelis.

The Syrians were already in the Lebanon, having sent in a battalion on 1 June 1976, and on 28 September they commenced an assault on the dug-in positions of the PLO. Although Bashir's appeals at meetings with Israelis would be strewn with talk of apocalypse and 'the Lebanon in mortal danger', the political truth which mattered was that the

Franjiehs had strengthened their position in the Lebanon by replacing the presidency just ending for Suleiman, by an understanding with the Syrians. The forces of that country would now make an attack upon the generally hated PLO. An agreement reached in Riyadh gave the Syrian presence and current enterprise legitimacy with their immediate Arab neighbours. Meanwhile the ostensibly impartial Syrian peacekeepers took care not to disarm the Maronite militias along with the Palestinian forces. What was popular in the country and thus good for the Franjiehs was clearly against the interests of government of the Lebanon by the Gemayels.

For this next period Bashir was alone (with even his father Pierre extremely cool). He was the opponent of the accepted Syrian–Maronite alliance and the advocate of a seemingly inopportune Maronite–Israeli combination. His talent may be measured in terms of his ability to exploit the weaknesses of this position. Israel had been tentative and measured in the days when she would have been more welcome as an intervener. With most of the Maronite command content to have the Syrians come in, Bashir, consistently sceptical about the Damascus connection and as consistently a visitor to Tel Aviv, was correspondingly valued more highly by Israelis, including some very senior ones. He was to become the ally of the Minister of Defence and the protégé of the Prime Minister. He also made himself genuinely popular with his own militia, gradually acquiring qualities of inspirational leadership not suspected when he had worn a mask at shipboard meetings with Israeli intelligence, or been so stricken with *mal de mer* as to be sick in front of his furious father.

Bashir used his value to the Israelis to make himself attractive to them. With them and with his followers, he would talk of his revulsion at the corruption of the old Maronite leadership and of his yearnings for something better. Given the perfect truth of his charges, it was not necessary for his intentions to be tediously sincere. Outrage and yearning are useful commodities, proclamation of them always a good thing. But what he murmured to the Israelis about 'doing what you did in 1948', and imposing Maronite military dominance on the geographical whole of the country, carried more immediate conviction.

Meanwhile he prophesied during the trough of his influence that the Syrians would make themselves disliked, a safe prediction about almost any originally welcome interventionist force, as the British army in Northern Ireland, offered tea at first but later rioted against, could attest. The Syrians did their share of raping and pillaging and generally threw their weight around. The flush of gratitude receded and Bashir's earlier words came to look well. History, he had said, 'was rife with examples of armies which came to the aid of their neighbours in distress and stayed as immovable occupiers'. However, the Syrians couldn't do it all for themselves; it was necessary to pick a quarrel with them. This would involve his militia in warfare, an ambitious undertaking since the record of Christian soldiering in the Lebanon showed more aptitude for murder than for battle.

Bashir achieved something else at this time. Camille Chamoun, himself an inviter-in of foreign powers and a fomenter of war, admired, perhaps recognized as familiar, Bashir's tactics and in 1977 came down heavily in his favour. Not the least of his reasons was an instinct that Israel was now riper for involvement and that to join her and Bashir would be to join the winning side. A Gemayel–Chamoun alliance shifted power within the Maronite command, leaving Tony Franjieh as the too crudely committed client of the increasingly unpopular Syrians.

Conversations between Maronite leaders, Bashir most active among them, and the Israelis, were not a swift ripple of instant consultation, but took place and matured across a long period of time and were part of the political landscape inherited after the Israeli general election of 1977 by the Likud government and its leader, Menachem Begin, a man in whom rage and sentiment alternated like candy-stripes. Although he would sometimes rage at Bashir, he was capable of the elementary unwisdom of believing him. The patriotic, idealistic talk of Bashir paid a dividend of undeserved respect. Understanding Begin's historic preoccupation, he steered his own conversation over and again to the word 'genocide' and its alleged imminence for the Maronites. Begin convinced himself firstly that the Maronites *were* in danger of elimination, secondly that Israel should not let that happen; so convinced, he was able to persuade himself that such chivalry was in Israel's practical interest – a rationalization of sentiment into self-service. But to win over Begin (and his more sceptical military advisers) conclusively, Bashir had to prove himself, to take unwelcome military action; in this he would be doing something awesome, committing Arab troops to fight with Jews against Arabs.

The opportunity came with Begin's first and limited move (called Operation Litani), against PLO camps in the south of Lebanon menacing Israel and themselves counter-menaced by the autonomous Christian captain, freelance and candid ally of Israel, Major Saad Haddad. Bashir's militia were no actual *use* to Haddad or the Israelis against the Palestinians. Most of the eight hundred men sent turned round and went away shortly after arriving, but even so slender a contribution amounted to two useful gestures: one of goodwill to Begin, another of defiant autonomy to the rest of the Maronite establishment.

At the same time, Bashir sought, as economically as possible, to pick his quarrel with the Syrians. It was a modest harassment, mostly a matter of laying mines and a little light sniping. But it was directed at forces accepted into the country by the legal government of the new President, Elias Sarkis, in consequence of an international agreement ratified at Riyadh. Meanwhile Haddad, who had done proper fighting, was threatened with trial for treason.

Bashir Gemayel was not now a man to burst into tears or throw up or show the qualities of a child. No action taken, whether it concerned the Israëlis, the Palestinians or the Syrians, mattered except in so far as it affected the power of the Gemayel faction within the uneasy Cosa Nostra of Christian politics. Bashir linked his diversion against the PLO and his wooing of the Begin government with an essay at the hinterland of Tripoli, traditionally held by the Franjiehs. The former president, Suleiman Franjieh, angry at such bargain-hunting, had walked out of a meeting of the Lebanese Front which aspired to contain all the Christian groups, and minor fighting was taking place among militias. All this provided a perfect pretext for a major coup.

Following the death of an individual Phalange member in a skirmish with the Franjieh troops, Bashir ordered that Tony Franjieh's house should be surrounded, ostensibly in pursuit of the killer. Hundreds of Phalangists, more willing for such action than for dangerous war with Palestinians, complied. And when Franjieh refused to surrender the fugitive, the house was attacked and Franjieh, his wife, children and servants slaughtered.

To kill an opponent may often be the most effective way of dealing with him; and since Franjieh would have resisted Bashir's drive for the presidency of Lebanon, as he had opposed an Israeli occupation, his erasure had superficial attractions. But the sponsor of Syrian involvement in Lebanon was mourned and regretted by his patrons, whose distress took the form of immediate military action. Commandos were brought into Beirut by the Syrians, other Syrian soldiers were fired on by the Christians and President Assad issued an ultimatum threatening to clean the Christian militias out of their strongholds in east Beirut by shelling them. Bashir with a flurry of operatic tears and admission of his people's inability to withstand a single Syrian division, attempted to threaten the Israelis with the consequences of his own calamity. Sensible men in Israel, General Gur and Ezer Weizmann, Commander-in-Chief and Minister of Defence respectively, observed that it was his quarrel and he had started it. Mr Begin, whose passionate partisanship kept him at a distance from the category of sensible men, felt an obligation even to assassins and authorized a threatening flyover by Kfir jets of the Israeli air force.

The Christians, who at all times gave the impression of an assembly of imperious cuckoos, were outraged that the planes were not used to bomb the Palestinians ('Christian', as I have said, is here a term of art). But even without that extra benediction, Bashir had done extremely well. The Syrians took the Israeli intervention seriously and ceased their action for the time being. Israel was further advanced into Lebanese affairs than had ever seemed likely, and, the full measure of Bashir's greatness, a gangland murder had been made the occasion for an international incident with the chief regional power stepping in on behalf of the delinquent. However, for the Lebanon and its people as a whole, the manoeuvre was less successful. Hafiz Assad of Syria, also a great man, that is to say one tinged at no point by compunction, shifted his attention from Beirut to the remoter mountain districts of the north where he occupied territory, notably in the Mount Lebanon area, traditionally a citadel of the Christian faction. After ineffective resistance by the militia, tens of thousands of Lebanese Christians were driven out of their homes. Bashir's triumph took a highly modified shape.

The essentially domestic nature of the conflict was underlined a year later in 1979 when an ambush intended for Bashir, and likely to have been ordained by the Franjiehs, killed instead his eighteen-month-old daughter Maya. Bashir was also inconvenienced by the intractability of the Chamoun faction. The Israelis, looking for sensibly organized allies against the PLO, advised again and again that the militias and their leaders should integrate. As advice for the organization of a real army this was impeccable, but to urge the reconciliation for administrative reasons of people most familiar with each other's throats was downright unworldly. Fighting broke out between the subfactions of Christianity. Bashir responded in the way he understood best, a massacre. He mounted a surprise attack on the headquarters of the Chamoun militia, the Tigers, killing eighty of them and narrowly missing their commander Danny Chamoun (luckily away with a mistress at the time). Like many acts of abject villainy, it worked extremely well. The Tigers broke up as an independent force. Danny went to France, some of his followers submitted and joined the Phalangists, others walked away from militia activity as too exciting. With two smaller military groupings, the Organization and the Guardians of the Cedars, suddenly recognizing that calls for integration had not been premature, Camille Chamoun himself was swiftly reconciled to the winning side. His son had been humiliatingly exiled, the independent power of the Chamouns had been broken, but a sum of £1 million was paid to the Chamouns in compensation. Camille Chamoun had been defined by Anwar es-Sadat and lived up to the definition.

By any assessment of a man rising by crime, Bashir Gemayel was doing rather well. He had concentrated all the power of his divided side into his hands. One opponent had been murdered, another had been driven out by surprise attack, and an ally had been acquired who was vastly stronger than the Lebanese Christians or any of their enemies. The Palestinians had been restrained and driven on to the defensive. Admittedly, this had been done by the exertions of Tony Franjieh's allies, the Syrians, but Tony, usefully dead, was in no position to take the credit. Admittedly, his murder had given the Syrians the pretext for taking payment in kind by the occupation of Mount Lebanon. But the losses of the Lebanon as a country were more than compensated for by the personal gains of Bashir, now sharply defined as his threefold-occupied country's dominant figure.

Elevated by the exertions of his allies on major battlefields and by tommy-gun persuasion at the domestic level, he appeared at his apogee less like a miniaturized General Franco than a more ideological Lucky Luciano. Part of Bashir's charm was the blatancy of his self-regard coupled with a gentlemanly ability to patronize those who had raised him up. And, owing everything to the Jews, he managed to retain a tinge of graceful and tempered anti-Semitism. One debt for weapons had been cancelled by Menachem Begin to the annoyance of the Israeli Ministry of Finance. It was made clear that the favour could not be repeated. 'Begin and Sharon', he observed of the men who had invented him, 'were not schooled by the Jesuits as I was. And they are certainly not patrons of charity.'

This was nothing, however, compared with the smouldering loathing for the Jews of his father Pierre. Almost at the start, during the private negotiations with the Israeli Labour government, at a time when Syria and Tony Franjieh dominated the Lebanese scene, Pierre had been introduced to Yitzhak Rabin who was then Defence Minister. He made clear his unhappiness at having to take this crucifier's hand. 'I want to walk in Lebanon with my head held high as a Christian and an Arab. I have been forced to turn to you, but I am filled with shame and dismay.' Much later, when talking with General Sharon and the vastly more reluctant Yehoshua Saguy, head of intelligence, Pierre Gemayel again expressed his natural distaste. What would be the attitude of a Phalangist government if Israel went all the way to Beirut and drove the Palestinian terrorists out (Sharon was thinking in terms of peace treaties, recognition and accords of the Camp David sort)? 'We are part of the Arab world. We are not like Haddad. We are not traitors.' 'You see,' murmured Saguy in Hebrew, 'no matter what we do for them, in the end they'll turn right back to the Arab world.' Machiavelli's observations on the inutility of gratitude as a bargaining-counter are neatly summed up by that exchange.

To return to Bashir, his ultimate step, once Israel had been involved, first in minor incursions and then in a full-scale military invasion, was to seek supreme office in his country. Showing a grave regard for the constitutional proprieties and the legal term of the current President, Elias Sarkis, Bashir set about giving his street domination and influential friendships due legal form in the presidential elections of 1982. The realization of that ambition was intertwined with the continuing struggle with the Palestinians, still present in force in west Beirut, and the Syrians, firmly settled into north Lebanon.

Israel was at this later date deeply committed. A minor punitive incursion had, as set out in chapter 1, become a siege of the Palestinians at the end of a war conducted across most of the Lebanon. (It had been conducted alone, since hoped-for co-operative action from the Phalange had been almost non-existent.) However, the siege of the Palestinians would in due course produce spirited Phalangist exertions – the massacre of the occupants of two Palestinian refugee camps, Sabra and Shatilla, a vicarious ignominy which would end Israel's long chapter of involvement. Being blamed by the Christian Lebanese was simply the alternative to being blamed *for* them!

The election itself took place in a parliament building from which the Israeli guns could be clearly heard, something which gave opponents of Bashir a sound pretext for boycotting the vote. Bashir was the most powerful man in the Lebanon, but election was not certain since those who disliked him did so with much vigour. The Muslims of west Beirut declared against him and his large bloc. They were joined in this by other Muslims from Tripoli and the northern Bekaa Valley, and those Christians who cherished the memory of Tony Franjieh. They called a boycott on the pretext of the Israeli soldiers cruising around the sovereign parliament, but also with a view to denying a quorum. The easy part of Bashir's game concerned Camille Chamoun, who in his old age talked about a personal candidacy and who was dissuaded in the customary way: an assurance of cabinet jobs for his nominees and hard cash. One option for Bashir was to change tack and have his bloc vote for an extension of the presidency of the outgoing Sarkis in return for his own appointment as Prime Minister. Under the Lebanese constitution (a contradiction in terms), at the end of a president's legal term and in the absence of a presidential election, the Prime Minister automatically acquires presidential powers though not the title. The Israelis confined themselves to a clear intimation of the preferences of the occupying guarantors, heavy hints to Shiite delegates from the Israeli-policed south and some nimble transport assistance (a helicopter for a delegate jumping the right way).

When Bashir was elected on 23 August with 57 parliamentary votes out of 63, some Israeli troops in sovereign Lebanon joined in the celebrations of the Phalange firing ammunition into the air. President Bashir Gemayel informed an Israeli delegation: 'Personally I shall always be with you. Politically, however, I shall opt for my father's line.'

In Israel the Prime Minister saw the election of his protégé as an opportunity for a peace treaty and concomitant recognition of the Israeli state. This was made clear at a meeting with the new President on 30 August at Nahariya in Israel. For a start, Begin wanted an official presidential visit to Israel; that is, he expected that Bashir, having had everything done for him, should make his sacrifices in turn, giving Israel the same relationship it enjoyed with Egypt and making the Lebanon as popular with the rest of the Arab world. It was a high return to ask, but the investment had been considerable: the defeat of the Palestinians and the imposition on the Lebanon of Israel's candidate. Bashir returned the vague and woolly answers of a very clear mind. On a peace treaty, he alone could not decide such matters. There were government and political institutions in the Lebanon to be involved. (The nice observation of constitutional legality is a common refuge of those who have risen to power by killing people.) The Lebanese government would continue to move in the direction of a treaty, but the hasty signing of one was neither wise constitutionally nor in the interests of security.

What Bashir wanted was to get the Palestinians out of the Bekaa Valley where they were holed up, and the Syrians out of the north where they had come after the murder of Tony

Franjieh. What Begin wanted was a peace treaty and a state visit, both signifying the Lebanon's detachment from the all-Arab commitment against Israel. Moves towards neither were forthcoming. The meeting was unfruitful though Bashir expressed his vague desire eventually to appear before the Knesset. How the debate between patron and client, between the gnarled oak and the python in its branches, would have developed can only be guessed at. Bashir Gemayel would never test the limits of ingratitude at the Olympic level he merited. His life, which in its early thirties had met two of the three adjectives of Thomas Hobbes, was about to complete the set.

After the Nahariya talks with Begin, Bashir had been angry with the Israelis for patronizing him and for making demands and talked about severing his links with them, but nothing had changed. He still sought the Palestinian expulsion and his militia had earlier, before the election, driven them out of the refugee camp near the Christian village of Mia Mia by burning down living-quarters. Looking to larger things in the future, he met his vital ally among the Israelis, General Ariel Sharon, in a Beirut restaurant on 12 September – a meeting for which the general had absolutely no authorization – and spoke of cleaning out all Palestinian camps from south Beirut, converting them into a zoo, 'putting the Palestinians on to air-conditioned buses' (an update of earlier population-shifting transport), and sending them over the Syrian border. 'By 15 October,' he said, 'there won't be a single terrorist in Beirut.'

On 14 September a detonator was operated by one Habib Tanious Shartouni. He was a well-known Phalange loyalist, a cousin of Pierre Gemayel's aide-de-camp, and had a sister living below the apartment in which Gemayel was speaking to a Phalange Young Women's branch meeting. He was also, like Mrs Flower, the neighbour in Auden's poem 'James Honeyman', the agent of a foreign power. This was Syria, later President Bush's respected ally, whose intelligence contact had instructed Shartouni to assassinate Bashir Gemayel.

All sorts of consequences flowed from Bashir's death: the massacre of Palestinian women and children at the Sabra and Shatilla camps, the tainting of Israel with that expression of Christian spontaneity, and the defeat of Begin's and Sharon's large ambitions in the Lebanon. The brutal conduct of Bashir's followers destroyed the link which the object of their grief had constructed. The life of Bashir, lived at all times perilously and ending in the assassination he had gaily practised, was, in the way of all such careers, successful until it failed, brilliant until it was dimmed out; it was murderous, greedy, self-preoccupied, morally non-operative and provincial. But it was the career of a clear-sighted, vigorous politician serving narrow ends by the brilliant exploitation of partners immeasurably stronger than either himself or the country in which he struggled by criminal means to dominate a minority element.

A census carried out by the Maronites, and suppressed by them, revealed later that the Christian community of the Lebanon were not the supposed 40–45 per cent of the total population, but only 30 per cent. The enterprise which collapsed in two piles of rubble, following Bashir's murder and that of the Sabra–Shatilla victims, had been constructed upon a half-inch base of credibility. The nerve and moral insolence which had drawn the Israelis into a chestnut-retrieving expedition on the strength of entirely fraudulent suggestions of Maronite strength were not light things. Bashir Gemayel was a charlatan as well as a killer, but he was a charlatan of international standing, neither lion nor quite fox, but a hyena of genius.

CHAPTER SIX A

The Prophet Unarmed: The high regard for legal means of General Charles de Gaulle in 1958

(*The Prince* IX)

The prophet armed, the prophet unarmed: they stand at the heart of Machiavelli's work as the great contrast, also the prime statement of his unrelenting realism. The prophet armed wins; the prophet unarmed loses. I deal with it in chapter 7 in the sinister modern context of armed forces, what Machiavelli called militias.

But armament can take subtler forms than a troop of para-military heavies. Government, if you know how to use it, *is* arms. And Charles de Gaulle, exiled by self and circumstances from power in 1946, had been unarmed for twelve gently diminishing years in his retreat of Colombey-les-Deux-Églises. His political grouping, the Rassemblement de Peuple Français, had failed to make a sustained impact and had developed unhealthy strains; and sadly, politics had worked tolerably well without his presence. Only the failure of others and, by extension, the failure of the France about which he spoke so magniloquently, would do the General any good. And we shall see, in the next two chapters, distinct accounts of de Gaulle: first, out of power but working towards it, second, however tenta-tively, holding power, and however circumspectly, using it.

It is not really odd to discuss Charles de Gaulle under the heading of Machiavelli's ninth chapter, the constitutional principality. For a start, de Gaulle had a delicate way of breaking the rules and staying within the law. Any corner he cut was in effect elegantly rounded off. But in his chapter 9, Machiavelli deals with rulers and their relationships with respectively the people and 'the nobles' (for whom we can read 'the politicians').

A principality, states Machiavelli, is created either by the people or the nobles according to whether the one or the other of these two classes is given the opportunity. The Florentine argument is that an incoming prince has to balance himself between the nobles who are astute and self-interested and will always try to back the winning side, and the people, less acute but more important. The people, he adds wistfully, are more honest, all they want is not to be oppressed while the nobles wish to oppress the people. Nothing so crude as the phrase 'playing one off against the other' is used, but it is at the heart of the argument. A man, he says, who has come in by the will of the people, must work to retain their favour; if he has risen without their support and by the influence of the nobles, he should then try to win them over. Nobles are both more threatening than the people and more dispensable. They are threatening because they will, unlike the people, be actively hostile to a prince and work against him, whereas the people, at worst, will be merely indifferent.

The purpose of Charles de Gaulle's life was to live above politics by single-minded application to politics. His hostility to the governments of the Fourth Republic (1946–58), coupled with his youthful dabbling with the Action Française of Charles Maurras, brought charges of Fascist leanings. In a country where Fascist tendencies in the officer class were somewhere between a commonplace and the norm, such accusations sprang easily to the lips of left-inclined commentators. But there was nothing commonplace about de Gaulle, and nothing Fascistic either.

We are afflicted today by political technicians whose minutely calibrated judgements spoil their mystique by being wrong. De Gaulle, cheerfully ignorant about economics, vague about social policy and out of step with consensual views on the United States, Europe and the Soviet Union, was capable of broad, uncalibrated judgements which were dead right. He did not believe in the received Cold War view of the Soviet Union as propagated by John Foster Dulles and accepted by every chancellery in Europe. The idea of a Manichean struggle of good against evil, the United States and its altar-boys against the devilish Soviet Union, struck him as ridiculous. He would withdraw France from NATO and emerge with more influence *vis à vis* the US than France ever had as a good member of the organization.

He was a nationalist but never of the frothing, soured embattled sort that Enoch Powell and latterly Margaret Thatcher became. He understood what George Orwell had argued earlier, that national feeling remains after it has been denounced, abhorred and legislated against. He had the odd, endearing knack of combining apparently old-hat romanticism with hard-eyed assessments of underlying realities. Significantly, he thought of the Soviet Union as 'Russia' and, with a shaft of truthful atavism, would refer to the German Democratic Republic as '*La Prusse*'. The term which suits him best is 'nationalist-realist'.

He could be depressingly narrow. He deplored European Community integration, but used the EC to extract for France a gross, prejudicial and economically distorting rig of agricultural markets and, when he had finished negotiating with Mr Heath, a quickly assembled fisheries policy every bit as rigged and self-interested. Without de Gaulle's influence, the reality of European institutions would have come nearer to their rhetoric and would not have caused the EC to lug around a burden of expensive fiefdoms. But France would have been a major loser and de Gaulle thought as a Frenchman in French terms, a posture not easily reconciled with what the French with heroic brass neck call *l'esprit communautaire*.

The de Gaulle of Machiavelli's chapter 9 was in conflict with politicians/nobles and seeking a long-term French interest which would be sustained by history. In the process he reminds one not just of Machiavelli, but of Cavour who said famously of his machinations in the 1850s, 'If we did for ourselves what we do for Italy, what scoundrels we should be.'

For a start, the politicians he swept aside were not in Machiavelli's terms seeking to oppress the people or showing more than customary selfishness. Nor did the men who had ruled France since his own irked departure in 1946 lack talents to compare with those of de Gaulle himself. Pierre Mendès-France, his mirror-image on the left, had shown what high, forceful democratic government could do in 1954–5 and he understood, exactly as de Gaulle did, the impossibility of allowing France to become enmired in Algeria. Jean Monnet and Robert Schuman had created the European Community, Antoine Pinay had demonstrated a sharply proficient grasp of market realism in French finance, Edgar Faure was the most exquisite fixer of his age. Essentially, the French economy, despite much melodrama and splashes of primary colours by way of inflation, was better than on course. It was making a sound to brilliant recovery, in marked contradistinction to its British rival, which was then complacently digging a pit for itself in slow motion.

By early 1957, however, when de Gaulle began to edge back closer to the political stage, the politicians and their system were held in a wide contempt – a matter of the people having a diminishing opinion of the nobles. Partly this was a result of the instability of the multi-party system, which gave governments under the Fourth Republic an average lifespan of eight and a half months. The English comedian Richard Murdoch had a little ditty around 1953:

They've called upon a farmer from the tip of Finisterre
He's the only living Frenchman who had not yet been Prime Minister.

A paperchase of governments does not make for dignity even if key ministries like Finance might be held longer by an individual than in Britain and essential policies broadly sustained across administrations. But a built-in destabilizer of France is its anti-democratic minority. More than twenty per cent of Frenchmen voted for the Communist Party which would remain, to the bitter end, loyal to a primitive Stalinism: loyal, as it were, to the Sacred Heart of Joseph. Meanwhile the elections of 1955 threw up Pierre Poujade – himself something less than a Fascist, as he was something less than a politician – who offered a refuge for the old anti-democratic dervishes who had disported themselves so joyfully under Vichy.

In 1945–6 the Communists had conducted something mistakable for a pogrom against the right, a folk revenge for things deeper-buried than collaboration with the Germans, but one in which for eighteen months the Communist party had wholeheartedly joined. The killings of 1945, whose image is preserved in Marcel Aymé's memorable novel *Uranus*, were a counterpoint to the massacres of 1871 when the Marquis de Galifet executed 25,000 working men in relays for involvement in the Commune. The France which the Fourth Republic and de Gaulle alike attempted to govern was not a happy place, not, in Mr Major's phrase, 'a nation at peace with itself'. To follow Machiavelli, it would be the function of de Gaulle to balance the people against the people under cover of rhetoric directed at the politicians. For by the late fifties not merely were the Communists still very strong under the grim-booted leadership of Maurice Thorez, but the right had a function and a focus far beyond the little-man, anti-tax, peasant's and shopkeeper's maunderings of Poujade. It had Algeria.

Chapter 1 has set out much of the Algerian imbroglio, but briefly, a little more. Algeria had been a French colony since conquest in 1830. The aspirations of its native population had been recognized by far-sighted administrators as far back as the thirties and after the war an independence movement, widely supported and turning quickly to extensive violence, had threatened the expulsion of France and her million or so white settlers. There was profound emotional French attachment to Algeria for reasons which were proclaimed to be hard-headed – France without her greatest colony would be nothing in the world! Should France then hang on to a thumping deficit by fighting an unwinnable war with increasingly unspeakable means? Various mystical things were said about *gloire, nation, patrie* and the rest of it, while dark-skinned men were wired to electric generators.

What the established Fourth Republic politicians were guilty of, most of all, was paralysis; they were guilty ultimately of *not* being in power. When that mob of settlers threw things at Guy Mollet, a prime minister who, by the rickety standards of France, enjoyed something like a workable majority, he reversed his policy, and cycled back. By nervous drift, a policy was reached of fighting the Algerian nationalist rising because the government of the day (and its successors) were afraid of the *colons*.

The left-wing intelligentsia were against the war; a good many friend-and-neighbour countries were at best cool about it; the three sharpest political minds in France, Raymond Aron, Pierre Mendès-France and Charles de Gaulle, each believed that it was futile; and the fourth or fifth sharpest, Antoine Pinay, had the gravest doubts about it. But the French government and the pool of politicians of the conventional right and left, from which a prospective government was likely to be drawn, were not against it . . . nor at heart were they for it. In this, the politicians were very like the people. The war was exhausting, unattractive and had no credible prospect of being won. If ever dispensed with, its end would be welcome. It was a war that should not have been started but could not be stopped. For the people, what was lacking was the spirit of opposition to war which would animate great tracts of the United States during the later stages of the Vietnam conflict. Politicians and people alike lacked faith in what they did, but lacked the will to stop doing it. So against the government went up the idiot right-wing cry of 'Treason'.

There is something about the supporters of indefensible ends which urges them upon self-destructive courses. If Fort Sumter had not been fired upon and war sought and urged by those who cherished slavery as a birthright, slavery would not have been expunged from American law formally in 1863 and effectively in 1865. Soft words and dragging feet could have kept the institution intact for the rest of the century. Acts of war turned a debate which could have run sempiternally into a war which could only be lost. So within five years of the first conspiracies against the French state by advocates of *Algérie française*, Algeria would be Algerian.

Conspiracy was drawn from several quarters: members of the army, settler ultras – and Gaullists. The Gaullist lawyer Maître Biaggi had been vividly active early in 1956, stirring up the demonstrations that broke the nerve of Guy Mollet and cancelled the appointment of Georges Catroux as Governor-General. This sort of thing was not illegal, but it decisively set in motion the process that destroyed the Fourth Republic. In the same year, General Jacques Faure, a Gaullist soldier, engaged in conversations with serving officers and made draft plans for a military putsch against the governments in both Algiers and Paris. He communicated them to the Prefect of Algiers, Paul Teitgen, not his sort of company. (Teitgen a year later would resign out of disgust at the wholesale use of torture.) This was simple treason, if of the preliminary sort, and it was punished with thirty days' fortress detention. As an undertaking it was as futile as Biaggi's activities were fruitful. But it demonstrated the relationship of conspirators and office-holders. The activities of the one terrified the other.

Disaffection of the kind which would lead to outright sedition had its strongest roots amongst more intelligent company than the buffoon Faure. Most important was Jacques Soustelle, a former secretary-general of de Gaulle's political party, the RPF (Rassemblement du Peuple Français). This formidable intellectual was widely thought of as one of the leftish, socially conscious Gaullists; but he was also a man quietly and hypnotically fanatical and what might be called a democracy-sceptic.

Soustelle gathered a group around him called USRAF (with the making of acronyms there is no end), the Union pour le Salut et le Renouveau de l'Algérie Française, which he stuffed with reputable, high-sounding establishment figures including some elderly liberals. It also contained hard right-wingers of some practical experience, including Georges Bidault, once a respected, if pompous, middle-of-the-road, ex-Resistance, national figure now beginning the long but accelerating transition to unhinged putschist. There were also entirely serious politicians like Jacques Chaban-Delmas who was then nothing more startling than the current Minister of Defence. The purpose of the group was to organize committees of public safety throughout France with a view to setting up a national committee of public safety which would pave the way to de Gaulle's coming to power.

If all this was not treason, it was the assembled mechanics of treason. Simply by existing, it constituted a piece of unalloyed deceit. Among the friends and contacts of Chaban-Delmas was one Léon Delbecque (who died in 1992), also a Gaullist militant, whose particular utility was the excellence of his French Algerian credentials. The Gaullists lacked sympathy among the *colons* for the simple reason that most of the latter had favoured collaboration with Germany during the war and had given their hero-worship to another general, Henri-Philippe Pétain. But Delbecque became as febrile a little provincial patriot as he was a Gaullist. He buzzed among the settlers with two messages – '*Algérie française*' and 'General de Gaulle' – stressing the certain securing of the first by the advancement to plenary national powers of the second. Delbecque held for these purposes an actual post in government service as an information liaison officer in Algiers at the Ministry of Defence. To this he had been appointed by Jacques Chaban-Delmas. A strong government would have arrested and tried Delbecque for sedition; a strong government would have dismissed Chaban in heavily publicized disgrace. A strong government would have confronted General de Gaulle with the illegal activities of his close associates and publicly required him to explain. But a strong government was the last thing that existed in France.

The perfectly decent, economically and administratively competent cabinet-fodder in France in the late fifties had no will to live. Mendès-France, already out of office for ever, had enunciated that dictum that governing means choosing. And the last three cabinets of France did neither. They existed without giving proof of the fact. It was said of Félix Gaillard that weeks before the actual vote which brought his government down, he met the prospect of its defeat like a sick man embracing death. And Félix Gaillard, outstanding graduate of all the approved high-intelligence citadels of education, was in excellent health and thirty-eight years old.

The fall of the Gaillard government was provoked by the Sakiet incident, the bombing of Swiss and Swedish nationals during an illegal and bungled French cross-border raid from Algeria into Tunisia, about which the Prime Minister had of course not been told. Gaillard responded with the usual ministerial mixture of good sense tempered by apprehension. He deplored the 'reflexive xenophobia' of some his countrymen, but defended the notion of hot pursuit in principle and spoke sharply of Tunisia as a terrorist haven.

Characteristically of decent men in the middle, he offended everyone. The Tunisians withdrew their embassy (after the ambassador had made a call upon General de Gaulle), and shortly afterwards Gaullist members withdrew from the government to which they had been conspicuously disloyal, in protest at the Foreign Office's attempts to behave according to ordinary rules of legality. It had agreed to an international commission (of Sir Harold Beeley and Robert Murphy) reporting on border security and the avoidance of such incidents in the future.

Jacques Soustelle took the Gaullists into the 'No' lobby together with the Poujadists and the Communists (who were frying fish of their own). Horror at France's agreeing to the friendly offices of Britain and the United States was expressed by Michel Debré, another follower of de Gaulle more Gaullist than the General: 'Rather the good offices of General de Gaulle than the American, Murphy.' Debré, editor of a publication called *Le Courier de la colère* and of a pamphlet, 'Ces princes qui nous gouvernent', was identified with two things: General de Gaulle and '*Algérie française*'. As Prime Minister under the General after 1958, he would be obliged to choose between them.

Circumstances began to unravel the Fourth Republic in the spring of 1958. Not only was the Gaillard government opportunistically defeated, but its replacement was an unconscionable time a-forming. This was nothing new for the Fourth Republic (or the Third). Two or three of the *papabili* would conduct a stately dance of the bowing and retreating sort while enquiring of other parties if they could support a given mix of men and measures. The third time around, enough arms would be linked for Adagio to become Andante, the Hotel Matignon would be occupied and France would have a government again.

It was not a good system, encouraging both derision and a sense of the change not mattering very much. On this occasion, the rejection of the right-wing Bidault, as a spokesman for the bringers-down (the right bloc), was followed by that of René Pleven, through abrupt Socialist Party concern to distance itself from the policy it had steadfastly followed for thirty months. When at last a government had been put together, it was done by Pierre Pflimlin, the very decent, left-of-centre, Catholic Mayor of Strasbourg who offered business very much as usual. But at the same time, the FLN, the main armed Algerian militant nationalist group, announced that it had murdered ('executed' is the usual impertinence), three French soldier hostages it had held for some time. This provoked riots of *colons* into which activist Gaullists plunged their hands up to the armpits. On the same day, the commander in Algeria, General Raoul Salan, previously thought to be apolitical and no darling of the *colons*, issued a statement of what the army would accept.

'What the army will accept' is a South American locution to strike terror into any constitutional politician. And what this army would *not* accept was a cease-fire inconsistent with its honour. The honour of the French army had last been a buzz-word during the Dreyfus affair, and much good that had done France. What would be consistent with that honour, and thus acceptable to General Salan, would be the laying-down of arms unconditionally by the FLN; under amnesty, their repre-sentatives would then enter a new and happier French and Muslim community. The objective might be touchingly naïve, but the statement was an assertion of political authority.

On the same day, 9 May, the four senior generals in Algeria plus the fleet commander passed through the retiring Lacoste a message for the Chief of Staff, General Ély. It announced that 'The French Army would, to a man, consider the surrender of this part of the national heritage to be an outrage. Its desperate reaction is unpredictable.' General Ély was asked to communi-cate to the President and Prime Minister 'our anguish which can only be assuaged by a government firmly resolved to keep the French flag flying in Algeria'.

Niccolò Machiavelli, whose military acquaintance was lim-ited to the class of candid hireling in the tradition of Sir John Hawkwood, salaried Captain-General of the Republic of Flor-ence, whose notion of what was acceptable and consonant with their honour could always be counted in cash, would have been appalled. Many things are tolerable in a commanding soldier, among them cupidity, vanity, defect of intellect and the desire, in the teeth of solemn contrary undertakings, to seize power.

What would have shocked Machiavelli would have been the sheer sanctimoniousness of it all. General Salan had been trained, hired, remunerated and promoted. His job was to obey orders or alternatively to betray his undertakings and attempt a coup. What was not, in his own phrase, 'acceptable' was that he should prattle of honour – and worse, think that he meant it.

Salan had gone to Algeria as a dull, competent, conscientious duty-doer whom the paranoid settlers had taken for an enemy and tried to kill. Shots intended for him at his desk had killed his assistant. He did not start as an adventurer minded to overturn the established government, nor was he a natural far-rightist fallen among friends. He would end as a half-crazed putschist on the run and ultimately in real danger from the unforgiving de Gaulle, of the firing-squad. But Salan, unlike Charles de Gaulle, was an honest soldier. Or to refine things, he was a bureaucrat unable to cope with the emotional excess of the mob.

The mob here is something more than a literal howling crowd, though that was present in full. The mob included the buzz of opinion in European circles, in the right-wing press, papers like *L'Écho d'Alger*, edited by de Sérigny, a former Pétainist who was about to call for de Gaulle as national saviour. The rage and fear of the Europeans of Algeria communicated itself to the men sent to save them. Wills, strong because frantic, subjected weaker ones which, rationally and at a hygienic distance, would have rejected their demands. The process of unreason and hysteria does not figure strongly in Machiavelli because of his exaltation of the rational, and because the princes to whom he addressed himself never envisaged a situation in which mob and rulers would be swept along together. When Machiavelli talked of 'the nobles' and 'the people', his attitude to the people was kindly if patronizing. They intended no harm and wished only not to be oppressed.

The people, defined here as the French population of Algeria, certainly feared being oppressed, being murdered was one form that such oppression would take. But they were equally keen to

do a full quota of oppressing themselves. The option of conciliation, of drawing Arab Muslim Algerians into a decent share
of political power jointly with the settlers, would never have
worked. But at the anguished and furious insistence of the
colons, it was never even tried. Terrible Muslim killings of
Europeans had been met with European killings of Muslims,
just as terrible and in larger numbers. 'The people' in this case
was no innocent wanting a quiet life; it was a collective version
of one of Machiavelli's nobles. It thought with its stomach
muscles and its clenched hands, thought entirely in terms of
having, holding and not letting go, and of the continued
oppression of those who, given the chance, would indeed have
oppressed in their turn.

The actual 'nobles', defined as the conventional politicians of
France, might not be very brave or decisive. They might, like
Félix Gaillard, have almost given up the ghost and the will to
political existence. They were men upon whom life had recently
made fierce impressions which lingered afterwards in their
features and actions. But they were no oppressors, except of the
Algerian Muslims in response to the requirements of 'the
people' who had demanded such oppression. They were led by
this oppression into the condoning of systematic electric torture
(as well as giving more happy endorsement to many thoughtful,
creative, well-digging, food-distributing, skill-training enter-
prises). Such undertakings were conducted by devoted Arab-
speaking French officers who represented, often in the same
man, two sides of the French military – and France.

But these inert, passive men were not the nobles with whom
de Gaulle would have to deal when he did come to power. The
new nobles would be his own active supporters, the Debrés, the
Delbecques and – both late and tentative – the military, the
Salans, the Massus, as well as the *colons* and their leaders, de
Sérigny, Lagaillarde and the rest of them, plus assorted Fascist
types riding the Gaullist whirlwind in France.

The irony was that while Gaullists moved smoothly around

Algiers, assuring the locals and the military that their hope lay in General de Gaulle, General de Gaulle had, in his private but candidly given discourses, left no doubt of his understanding of Algeria. His door at Colombey-les-Deux-Églises was always open to reputable, useful or interesting figures. One for whom he had a warm regard was the anti-Communist but left-wing Socialist André Philip who, with more moral courage than most, would oppose his return to power. Philip had been in Algeria when de Gaulle had been at the headquarters of the Free French during the Second World War.

The view of the man for whom Léon Delbecque burrowed like a mole in the ground and who Soustelle, Debré and the whole pack thought would rescue *l'Algérie française* was that 'the only recourse is via the independence of Algeria by stages, if possible in association with France.'

Philip observed that in the revolt now brewing de Gaulle's name would be used by the rebels. De Gaulle spoke as Machiavelli would have wished: 'If there is a government it will govern and the army will obey. The army only rebels when it is frustrated in its natural instinct to obey. If there is no government, the army will assume power in Algiers. And as for me, seeing that there is no longer a State, I will assume power in Paris in order to save the republic.' But then, said Philip, de Gaulle would never be able to proclaim the independence of Algeria. What followed in reply was de Gaulle at his finest, grasping essentials, keeping his nerve long and massively, getting everything right and proposing comprehensive perfidy.

'Come on Philip. Don't be naïve. You have lived in Algiers as I have. They are all noisy people. The only thing to do is to let them make a noise. As for the military, I shall remain calm while their leaders destroy each other. With what remains, I shall do what I want with promotions and decorations.'

It is superb. Here are the people; here, among the military, are the nobles and here, lucid, calculating and wonderfully good-humoured, is the prince. But because de Gaulle did have such foresight does not mean that he knew what would happen or that what did happen would deal court cards to him. He had down moments when he reflected on a different course. He told the MRP MP, Robert Buron, like Pflimlin a leftish Catholic, 'It is too late . . . The situation cannot be stabilized for several years and I shall then be too old. The French must first plumb the depths before they can reach the heights.' But the greatest strategist can only make a guess at what his tactical chances will be. De Gaulle stayed alert, informed and ready, so that if the chance did come, he would know exactly what to do with it.

Power would be put in his hands by the mobs and military of Algiers – the two groups now hardly distinguishable from one another – making a great noise; and Gaullists who would have died of grief to hear the General's conversation with André Philip were at work orchestrating the takeover. The news of the three 'executions' had started a riot, Salan had made his statement, the departing Robert Lacoste had said something about 'another Dien Bien Phu', the French surrender in Indo-China, and events were rolling. A group of non-Gaullists, 'the Seven' led by the student activist Pierre Lagaillarde, made the immediate running by sacking the American Cultural Centre before bringing their mob along to the Gouvernement-Général (Government House in British colonial terms). They took it with military police and parachutists looking on.

So far the Gaullists had nothing, while back in Paris Pflimlin at least had a majority – 274 to 129 – to form a government. As Frank Giles, historian of the Fourth Republic and *The Times* Paris correspondent at the time, puts it, that government could join the rebels, fight them, or send for de Gaulle. Pflimlin did two contradictory but not absurd things: he ordered the army to obey and put all power in the hands of Salan. Meanwhile General de Gaulle on a visit to Paris was telling his publisher that with only the seventh and last chapter of volume III of his memoirs to write, he would be able to deliver it by 15 August for publication in October (such publishing!). That elegant volume was to be delayed by a year. And the Mongénéral, as sycophants called him, as so often, was lying.

A vote of confidence was sought for the government, and by 405 to 165 it was given. But politicians were coming, in increasing numbers and in important places, to feel that the larger conflict was lost and that they must treat with de Gaulle as the only man who could call off the dogs. That it was he who had called them on and he who would lock them up in kennels for good was merely irony. The other option was a mass mobilization of public opinion against the putschists. But that involved putting a weapon into the hands of the Communists, at that time about a fifth of the electorate, hard-handed Stalinists with a trade-union arm, not actually much more agreeable in the streets than the frantic Fascist captains of Algiers. Paul Johnson, writing fervent left-wing copy for the *New Statesman*, might speak of the need to arm the miners of the Nord. Official people faced with the prospect of civil war preferred Mongénéral. As Pleven, the Foreign Minister, put it to a midnight meeting of ministers early on 28 May, what power did the ministers of the Republic have that they could defend? The Minister of Defence was not obeyed by his troops, the authority in Algeria of the Ministry for Algeria was long gone (had been gone since the episode of the tomatoes thrown at Mollet) and the police did not answer to the requests of the Ministry of the Interior.

Pflimlin and the President of the Republic, Coty, postponed the actual resignation of the Prime Minister only because they wanted the transition to be fully legal and in due form, involving a decision of the Chamber of Deputies.

Meanwhile de Gaulle was being told by the representative of the putschists-in-waiting, a General Dulac, that if his way to power were barred in the Chamber, 'Resurrection', code name for full dress military insurrection, stood ready in reserve. According to Dulac, de Gaulle, while expressing a distinct preference for not being the obvious nominee of the coup and preferring to descend, as if by baroque stage machinery, at the command and need of France, nevertheless sent Salan the message that 'what he has done and is going to do is for the good of France'. Delbecque, who was present, allegedly expressed surprise that he should line up with the threats. But it was late, the crisis could well dissolve. The dispassion of the de Gaulle who spoke to Philip was challenged by the anxiety of the morose de Gaulle who spoke to Buron. Either way it was a trickiness beyond the dreams of Richard Nixon and astonishingly at odds with the grandeur to which Mongénéral made recurring reference, commonly aspired and which, from time to time, he achieved. Beneath the Corneillian manner, the remarks were cheap Bolivian putschism.

Further allegations suggest a deeper commitment to illegality. General Jouhaud would later claim that the men of Resurrection made contact with Colombey-les-Deux-Églises. General Nicot, an air force general, approached de Gaulle through Pierre Lanfranc, one of his staff, to say that the General Staff were unwilling to start Resurrection without his approval. Lanfranc at the phone conveyed complete agreement. Admittedly the evidence depends upon an intermediary and de Gaulle was masterful in his ambiguity. Admittedly Lanfranc, a Gaullist loyalist, would deny the conversation completely, just as General Nicot would reaffirm it. One or other of two upholders of 'honour' was lying in his teeth. But the question at issue was very clear, and the means to choose legality were at hand in a simple withholding of support. However his remarks were phrased, General de Gaulle in that dialogue will have understood that he could stop or start treason. He did not stop it.

Resurrection, having been delayed, was now timed for 30 May and de Gaulle had another ally, President Coty, a man a little way above mediocrity. Not quite above reproach during the wartime period, Coty was charming and amusing: 'I have been made President because I was having a prostate operation at the time of the EDC debate';* but he was not the tough fighting

* The European Defence Community, involving a rearmed Germany. An American imposition, it split France in 1953 from the nave to the chops.

intelligence that his predecessor Vincent Auriol had been. About his going there was much dignity and some passive wisdom, but it was very much a matter of graceful debility. The vacuum which his departure would create, so helpful to de Gaulle, might be regarded as the logical conclusion of his melancholy presidency. The threat of ending his presidency was aimed at those unwilling to end the republic. If Charles de Gaulle had been as bad as the company he was keeping, if he had kept faith with his sponsors and made a republic acceptable to settlers and treasonable army officers, Coty might be remembered with Bazaine, who abandoned Metz, garrisoned, provisioned and armed, to the Prussians in 1870. As it was, the General's grand betrayal of the men who had re-created him cast the politic acquiescence of Coty into a long, generous light.

A public demonstration had brought 150,000 people out on to the streets in defence of the Republic, led by the consistent left democrats, but with the Communists an unwelcome presence. It was not bad but it was not enough: not enough to frighten, enough to be called frightening, less a prospect of resistance than a pretext for talking about popular fronts and Communist entry.

A second St-Cloud encounter found a de Gaulle whose discourse counterpoints his alleged remarks to Lanfranc and Dulac. The spur of plotters became a man warning against plotters. He wished to prorogue the Assembly for a year while submitting his constitution to referendum. When this was cavilled at by the Speaker, Le Troquer, de Gaulle said with an unbecoming mixture of self-pity and blackmail, 'If parliament agrees with you, I will have no alternative but to leave you to have things out with the parachutists and go back into retirement, with grief as my companion.'

Coty responded in his decent way by recognizing that the time for hole-and-corner diplomacy was over and resolving that he would openly send for de Gaulle to form a government as a prelude to constitutional change. He would also go himself whatever happened and in the event of de Gaulle not proceeding he would, following the rules of the Fourth Republic, make way for the Speaker. Having failed to blackmail directly, de Gaulle had the chance to provide the hovering threat of parachutists seizing the airports and the radio with a lining of charm. He took it brilliantly, inviting the Socialist leadership to Colombey and putting on his best moderate, responsive self; the genial, cynical de Gaulle was always better value than his Britannicus act. He also cycled back a long way from his initial anti-parliamentary insistences. Governments under his republic would, he now undertook, be answerable to the Assembly; he did not wish to function as the representative of committees of public safety, and as for Algeria, he hoped for federal links of some sort. It flew in the teeth of what the men of Algiers wanted and what they expected of the General. It was not extravagantly distant from what he would deliver, though whether the relatively parliamentary and democratic regime which the Fifth Republic has been, is quite representative of the General is another matter.

But it was enough for the Socialists, just. By 77 votes to 74 their caucus approved support for de Gaulle as Prime Minister. And it was to parliament that de Gaulle came on Sunday 1 June to make his speech as prospective premier. It was successful, and he was elected by a vote of 320 to 224 with half the Socialists and Radicals voting for him. It was a strange achievement. A few weeks earlier, support for de Gaulle, beyond his own regular supporters, would have been very thin. The General was respected and liked, the Assembly not vastly popular. But politics for most people has to do with going on with the present state of affairs. There was no majority or anything like one for a change of regime in the absence of crisis.

It was the *presence* of crisis which made de Gaulle possible. His assumption of power had been facilitated by the surrenders of the President of the former Republic and acceptance of his arrival by half the Socialist party and by a majority of the Assembly, all in the circumstances of soldiers waiting to seize power by armed force. Though never a prude, de Gaulle disliked the notion of *naked* force. His coming to power was a coup, but it was decently if hurriedly dressed in parliamentary and constitutional form. The form was to matter to the people who resisted de Gaulle, both those voting against him and those who insisted on the Assembly's role.

The General was the nominee of a bristling and insistent military and colonial right with its mainland and civilian allies. That he did not become a South American-style *caudillo* or look across the Pyrenees for inspiration had many reasons. But de Gaulle was a politician before everything; his authoritarian impulses mattered less than his instincts for manipulation and cajolery. Machiavelli, born to blood and sudden knives, would have found him congenial but rather domesticated. The republican elements remained strong in defeat. De Gaulle, born in 1890 and into a military–conservative caste, was too fly to be the prisoner of his generation, his near–allies or the prejudices of either; but his acceptability to forces rash and ready enough to pull the house down was what enabled him to inherit it.

In his coming struggle in Algeria, de Gaulle would have those forces as embittered enemies, the republicans as allies; the state he was to devise would mellow so much into an intelligent amendment of the Fourth Republic that the temptation exists to call it the Four-and-a-halfth. But the balance of people and nobles, the Machiavellian end, had been achieved at the outset, and across eleven years of broad presidential domination would be sustained; the decently dressed coup was a means, and, like all discreditable means, would be made light of. Victory can afford to be more fastidious about its ancestors than about its allies.

The prophet was after all now decently armed. So equipped with the equivalent of guns and swords, he was placed both to govern *and* to choose. Armament implied not just new strength but improved quality of prophecy-fulfilment, the prospect of doing very much more of what he actually wanted to do.

The Prophet Armed: The delicate exercise of
power by General Charles de Gaulle after 1958

(*The Prince* IX)

Actually in power, de Gaulle faced the same problems as the
Fourth Republic politicians he had replaced and he faced almost
the same enemies. The army was affected both by the frustration
of its professional job in suppressing a revolt and raised in its own
esteem as a successful defier of legitimate authority. The
Europeans of Algeria were as fearful and threatening as ever; their
leaders, having bought Gaullism with reservations, saw it as a
probationary gospel and were ready very quickly to disbelieve.
De Gaulle also faced, in more fulminant mood than before, the
far left in the form of the Communist Party and a busy student
body, though whether either was good for more than the
sacrament of protest was doubtful.

What he did *not* have against him were the Gaullists, the likes
of Delbecque agitating among the French of Algeria and
proclaiming the name of some retired old soldier as the approved
hero upon whom conspirators should focus their efforts. Safe
from the Gaullists, de Gaulle did not have to struggle against de
Gaulle. He was secure from the opposition of both the wily,
ambiguous and elegantly duplicitous politician and the mystical
presence, the national monument subtly occluded by the mists of
frugal theatricality from close inspection. De Gaulle was, and
knew it, a sort of alternative monarch. To him attached, as well as
the admiration his talents and intentions deserved, vague and

reverent feelings appropriate to a man above politics – a monument, but a monument charged with the force to change and achieve things. He was highly conscious of this and spoke of the statue in *Don Giovanni*. Not that he pressed the point, for it is the function of the Commendatore's statue in that opera to take the miscreant by the hand and disappear with him down to Hell. The *châtiments* of Mongénéral were altogether milder and more constructive.

But just by being de Gaulle, the man above politics, he was paradoxically able to play rougher and dirtier politics than any acknowledged politician. The French of Algeria who had helped him to power lumped Communists, Radicals and conventional democratic politicians together as enemies (in much the same spirit that, once, Charles Maurras had denounced what he called the *métèques*). Although Algerian Europeans were heavily tainted by Vichy and collaboration, de Gaulle of the Resistance was yet thought of as a man of the right. He was a soldier and a patriot, was he not? He had fallen out with the system of electoral politics; the far left instinctively called him a Fascist. More fool the far left . . . and more fool the far right. It takes the left to betray the left and the converse is true. As soldier, patriot and scorner of the parliamentary system, he was given trust which would always have been denied to civilian non-nationalist parliamentarians leaning backwards to accommodate the settlers. The Europeans had pelted Mollet with tomatoes, they had hanged Pflimlin in effigy from a tree in a square in Algiers. De Gaulle they cautiously trusted; more fool them.

De Gaulle began his struggle in Algeria, like Guy Mollet, with a visit. It was a very different visit. Before he was through with the policy intimated that day to the quick-eared, they would throw worse things than tomatoes and their representatives would try to kill the General in stark reality. But he spoke to 30,000 submissive Europeans who willed themselves to think him on their side and were foolishly persuaded. His words on the occasion of that visit were characteristically

handsome (de Gaulle spoke a beautiful classical French untouch-
ed by jargon or American), and characteristically deadly:

> I have understood you. I know what has happened here. I see
> what you wished to do. I see that the road you have opened in
> Algeria is that of renovation and fraternity. I say renovation
> in every respect. But very rightly, you wished that this
> should begin at the beginning; that is to say by our institu-
> tions, and that is why I am here.

In the light of what de Gaulle subsequently *did* this paragraph
deserves analysis. The first three sentences contain no judgement of any kind, no approbation or blame. They are neutral
but, in the excitable, overcharged context could import an
approval never voiced and quite absent from the record. The
fourth sentence is conscious and deliberate waffle and flatly
untrue. The settlers desired entrenchment and racial supremacy.
But it contains in the flaccid, up-beat rhetorician's word 're-
novation' the peg for what he wants actually to do. In the fifth
sentence he takes his listeners – in the teeth of their likely real
wishes – into the idea of major change. After the semi-colon of
the sixth sentence he tells them that the goal-posts will be
moved and the pitch sown with broken glass. The 'institutions'
to which he refers can be read as the French parliamentary
democracy which they hate; so the observation wins approval.
Equally, it can be their own specific institutions as an ascend-
ancy in a colony. His listeners are left applauding a speech which
we now know told them that having understood them, he
found them wanting and that the walls behind which they stood
fighting must be pulled down. A breathtaking piece of draped
audacity, it was magnificent and it was war.

In the same speech he broached the question of the Muslims:
'From today there is only one category of inhabitant: there are
only whole-share Frenchmen . . .' The settlers had been
making noises about integration, about their status with the

Muslims as part of France. But it was never intended by them that Muslims, counted in statistically with France, should have equal French rights and powers. De Gaulle says to anyone listening that he means just that, proposing 'to open paths which until now were closed to many . . . give the means of living to those who did not have them . . . recognize the dignity in those in whom dignity has been contested . . .' That last remark was a cool observation on the racial triumphalism of the Europeans which even his ambiguous reference to a mother-land did not sweeten. It was possible, however, to understand in de Gaulle's words an intention to make integration real and generous. France would stay, the settlers would survive but an Algeria with two cultures, bound up by goodwill and reforms, would function honestly, across the sea but inside the nation. De Gaulle liked talking like this; it reflected his preferences in circumstances of perfect free choice. A generous nationalism appealed to him, one in which France behaved well and justly towards the peoples at its penumbra, treating them squarely, respecting their culture but soaking them in French ways.

A society in which good Muslims elected a Muslim mayor who also represented the *département* in Paris, a society in which responders to the muezzin could quote Du Bellay by the stanza was beautiful and desirable. But it was unreal at this stage and de Gaulle was never held back by unrealities. His deepest political secret was a cherishing of idealistic notions while practising the most accountant-like *realpolitik*; he was the poet of his own betrayals.

His next (and entirely practical) move was to vest a great deal of power in the army in the tricky and uncertain person of General Salan who was made Delegate-General with plenary powers. This served two purposes: it flattered a man with a great deal of irregular power by giving him the insignia and fetters of slightly sham official power, and after the destruction of authority on 14 May it put somebody in charge; and with the army, de Gaulle's writ, however imperfectly, did run. When the local Europeans, organized into their committees of public safety, voted through a rank Fascist demand for the abolition of all political parties, Salan was compelled by de Gaulle to repudiate it. The CPSs were in control of Radio Algiers; they aspired, under the lead of local rightists and of Gaullists of the stamp of Soustelle, to the exercise of power for totalitarian purposes on the mainland where they wished to make war on 'the princes of the system who hope to smother the revolution'. In all this, de Gaulle proved a different sort of Gaullist from Delbecque. The CPSs were told to obey the legal authority.

On Bastille Day de Gaulle strengthened the loyalty of the army by a confetti-shower of promotions and honours. He understood the idiot magic of what Harold Macmillan called 'a little something to wear under your tie'. The power vested and the honours distributed were intended to draw the army to de Gaulle; they were also meant to split the army from the settlers and their instruments, the committees of public safety on which army officers had freely sat. The danger from the CPSs would have been greatest if Army and Gaullist elements had remained active in them, giving wider authority to anti-democratic moves. Flattery and responsibility weaned soldiers away, while the local Gaullists, though very happy with the anti-democratic tone of the committees, became the victims of their own messianism. Bound to de Gaulle, as he never was to them, by a mystique of acceptance and obedience, the Gaullists failed to rally round the right at the precise moment when the General became the effective guarantor of conventional democracy, however amended and modified. Their neutralization left the CPSs nastier but less important, fulmination chambers rather than springboards for action against the state.

De Gaulle's policy drift was tested by a referendum on setting up a Control Commission, an alternative and legitimate source of authority. The positive vote was confused by FLN orders for Muslims to abstain. When de Gaulle said in response to the meaningless result that 'without any constraint . . . a fact as clear as the dazzling light of day . . . it engages France and Algeria to each other for ever', he was making a soothing noise.

The activities of fifteen months involved referendum, elections and a development plan, *le plan Constantine*, a thoroughgoing piece of social expenditure of which any socialist government would have been proud and which ironically, made appeal not just to the Muslim population who would benefit but to the army, parts of which had been as fully engaged on social work as had others on the application of torture. The General, now formally President of the Fifth Republic, also decreed wholesale clemency for FLN prisoners. He was balanced between Europeans (both those in Algeria and the right generally), who desired comprehensive integration, and the majority of Muslims who desired a sovereign independent Algeria. His predecessors of the Fourth Republic, faced with a similar impasse, had been the prisoners of these two sorts of intransigence and of the manifest willingness of enough army officers and Europeans of Algeria to overthrow the state. White Algiers wrote limits to what Paris might do.

Armed against such threats by his perceived political colour and marmorial status, de Gaulle armed himself further by considered and deliberate delay. His own constitutional changes provided a pretext for that delay in the shape of a series of votes, electoral and consultative. These created a simulation of activity which was garlanded by his own lofty, cryptic and mischievous pronouncements. But water which had been on the boil and which could have scalded the entire nation fell to a steady simmer. If the military, the Gaullists of Algeria and the indigenous white right had all worked together at the same time, another putsch – this time with unambiguous authoritarian purposes – would have been attempted, with a middling prospect of a general strike against it, followed by armed clashes between police or army and workers and the pre-conditions of a civil war.

The three elements of potential opposition did not combine

because de Gaulle kept them apart and out of schedule with one another. General Salan, who would later be drawn into assassination plots, was flattered with authority but only on de Gaulle's behalf. Before he could grow too mighty he would be wafted out of it to a ceremonial grand inspectorship created for his reception. Jacques Massu, the most intelligent, dangerous and formidable of the military, was eventually won over more as a de Gaulle ally than a Gaullist. (When there was a street threat from the student left in 1968 – *les événements* – it was upon his old friend the army commander, General Massu, that de Gaulle made a pointed call in Alsace.) Deprived of the backing of the army, the white right complained, passed resolutions, made threatening noises but lacked credibility as a force against the state. And this credibility was their citadel. Nobody from Mollet to Pflimlin had deferred to them out of affection or disinterested fairness. Their tragedy was to become, by slow but distinguishable degrees, less frightening and thus less attended to.

During this long period of crafted gradualism de Gaulle talked more and more to the Muslims with their interests in mind. Philip Williams and Martin Harrison, writing in the immediate aftermath of events, observe that he had begun to speak to 'Algerians', not something the settlers called themselves, and that his legend had become '*Vive l'Algérie et la France*'. In so fine a speaker of French the use of a conjunction does not occur by accident. He also took to speaking with open respect for the soldiers of the FLN – 'For the most part, the men of the insurrection have fought courageously' – and he began to speak of coming forward to negotiate 'under the white flag of parley'. The Algerian command was less than overwhelmed by the term 'white flag' and the Europeans were given no joy by 'negotiate'. That initiative came to nothing, but it put 'negotiation', a word from the index of prohibited thoughts, into the lexicon of debate in France. It also had the happy effect of making the settlers quarrel among themselves. They split into extreme and moderate factions. The pro-French Muslims, the Harkis, would become by degrees loosened from European tutelage. (The Harkis, incidentally, were not necessarily people to be dismissed as servile collaborators; genuine co-operation had its appeal and the FLN promised a brutally intransigent state.)

For a man chosen by settlers and their allies, de Gaulle was behaving with marked liberality. The Constantine plan was aimed at investment, education and housing. It expanded the best intentions of Mollet's Governor-General, Lacoste, who is remembered for his support of repression, but was a painstaking Socialist for all that. At £1.5 billion in the values of 1959, it involved planning ahead for the explosion in population and making some provision for the million Muslim unemployed. It was 'one-nation' politics, something remarkable across two countries. The *colons* might not care for such things, but would hardly start a rising against them; the loyal Muslims were made most loyal to de Gaulle; and the army, much taken with social care, was likely to be delighted.

At the same time, de Gaulle wanted elections and made it clear that he wanted fair elections and insisted on the army's guaranteeing such fairness. If this doesn't sound very Machiavellian, consider the reaction of the settlers. The main committee of public safety, wanting ideally no elections and certainly not fair ones, called a general strike throughout the province only to find that with its Gaullist members dissenting, they had to climb down in the face of army hostility. By behaving in an orthodox, decent-chap sort of way, it is possible in certain circumstances to split your opponents in the most satisfactory fashion, by a kind of virtuous guile.

The state of affairs at this point was one in which the settlers were being rapidly disabused about de Gaulle (more than that, actually – hopping mad as befitted paranoiacs finding that everybody *was* against them); the army was divided between its idealistic middle-rank elements in the field and its itchily ambitious commanders, but holding together uneasily for de Gaulle; and the non-insurrectionist Muslims in the middle were coming closer to de Gaulle than to local Europeans. At the same time the war was getting a rotten name, much as the American effort in Vietnam would do, not just with the protesting classes but with church witnesses, Catholic and Protestant, and other solid, dangerous people. The establishment of camps, as had happened with the British in South Africa nearly sixty years before, did nothing to improve the savour. Reports of summary executions were equally unengaging. The phrase, much used from Mollet and Lacoste onward, of *la mission civilisante* was now pregnant with more irony than could quite be coped with. At this time, relations with abroad – foreigners, the UN, Americans and the like – hit a very low point, with threats from the curmudgeonly Debré, de Gaulle's heavy, to break up NATO or the EEC as occasion demanded. Such a mood mattered less than it seemed to at the time; but as a symptom giving some idea of France's fraught and ratty condition, it did very well.

As for the FLN, they were embarrassed by that offer from the General that they should come 'under the white flag of parley' to negotiate. The ablest FLN leaders were in jail; the interim leadership was caught on the wrong foot and refused to respond. As for the words used, FLN and settlers alike stressed 'white flag'. People thinking in the longer term saw the principle of negotiation.

What mattered now was Humpty Dumpty's question, 'Which is to be master?' It always had. It always does. The generals were keener on political power than during their tentative earlier steps, but they were further away from power than they had been in the days of May, *Im wunderschönen Monat Mai*. Talk of negotiations, reprieves, and the sinuous duplicity of Charles de Gaulle, all distressed them. He was splendid at giving assurances – he would not actually say '*Algérie française*'. 'What is the political significance of it? That Algeria is French. Is it useful to say so, since it is so?' With that deadly avuncular charm which marked his Indian summer, de Gaulle observed that 'those who shout loudest for integration today are those who were formerly against it. What they want is to be given *Algérie de papa* but *Algérie de papa* is dead and if they do not understand that, they will die with it.'

Almost certainly what de Gaulle wanted from the Algerian mess was what he called *francisation complète*, a genuine form of integration, with Muslims as the local majority enjoying autonomous control but in association with France who would spend good money to advance it. It was the best solution, the truly enlightened one, but at odds with the nationalism and anti-colonialism of the day. If it could not be had, his conversation with André Philip shows him ready to fall back on the swift making of an end. Behind the Comédie-Française locutions, these were the options.

No one put things quite so plainly, but the idea was taking shape. The settlers were not subtle people, having no opponents, only enemies. Talk of de Gaulle being 'dealt with' went into currency. The generals were more restrained but unable to stay in line. The committees of public safety, so influential in May 1958 that the generals approved something of the same name to govern France, had degenerated within a single year into gatherings ringing with cries of 'de Gaulle to the gallows' and '*Vive Pétain*'. The General, hearing of such things a year after the days of May, would have expected nothing else.

The elections had produced from Algeria a mixed body of moderates and extremists, also a large number of Harkis. These were lately being less awed and significantly less trusty than had been intended by the *colons*, denouncing '*Algérie de papa* with its train of corruptions'.

De Gaulle played his hand long, allowing a new military operation, 'Binoculars', to be launched without the least belief that it would seriously matter, but glad to keep the army sweet with war therapy. To the army he talked of 'carrying on the job' and to the Muslims of 'peace'. For the moment he would ask too much of the FLN. His next overtures, made on his first visit as President, an office hugely enhanced under his new republic, denounced secession as 'improbable and disastrous'. He threatened an end to all French aid and maintenance of a firm hold on Saharan oil. The FLN should disappear, de Gaulle should be trusted to deliver his *francisation* and the rest of the Muslims would make a free choice of anything, including secession, for themselves by self-determination. They would make their choice in due, late course after the creation of local councils and authorities.

It wasn't going to happen that way, but the right was suitably furious. Georges Bidault, who sounded here very like Enoch Powell, denied that 'the nation' had the right to consent to amputation of territory. Phrases in use quoted by Williams and Harrison were 'surrender is on the march', 'little by little, the scuttlers are triumphing' and 'self-determination is the surrender of Algeria'. The FLN, after some delay, made a series of fierce objections to the self-determination referendum, but it left doors open and itself used the language of negotiation.

The effect of these moves in the autumn of 1959, and the next moves, was to push the generals and the Algerian settlers, now too late back on terms, into an infuriated illustration of their impotence. By January 1960 de Gaulle was to announce a further conference, this time at the Élysée. This was coupled with the banning of Bidault from Algeria. Jacques Massu, later to become so respectable, so *fils de papa* in his relationship with de Gaulle, gave an interview with a German newspaper saying violent things against de Gaulle's Algeria policy. Over the head of his armed forces ministries, de Gaulle insisted on his removal. On 24 January, a Sunday, a demonstration was called, not unlike the one in May 1958 which had had such consequences. The regulars of settler outrage gathered: the student leader Lagaillarde, now a deputy, de Sérigny of *L'Écho d'Alger* and an unpleasant man called Joseph Ortiz. The Harkis failed to turn out, indeed there was a pro-de Gaulle gathering of thousands in the kasbah. In another part of the country, a Muslim crowd shouting '*Vive de Gaulle*' was fired upon.

The demonstrators, having set up barricades, were obliged to stay. If concessions could be won from de Gaulle, they and their military friends would retain standing and influence; if not, not. No one understood this more clearly than de Gaulle and he conceded nothing. He was urged ardently, begged, by ministers and senior military men, to give some ground, and responded by broadcasting to defend the referendum question on self-determination – exactly what the demonstration at bottom was against. He also put a question to the army – did it choose to be 'an anarchical and derisory collection of military clans' or an army as he understood one? (In that question, M. Philip would have recalled his conversation with the General.) This challenge was coupled with some cool redeployment. Massu's own para-troopers, who had been policing the city and could be trusted in nothing, were replaced by another, more reliable division. Not for the first time, de Gaulle found friends on the left. A neat little one-day strike, that French speciality – good for making a point without loss of productivity – was called and registered a gratifying turn-out: a strike called by the unions in support of de Gaulle!

With de Gaulle's parliamentary party, the UNR, holding solid, any military thought of rerunning the last reel of 1958 was made to look silly. The next step for the General, never a man to waste time on magnanimity, was to clean out enemies and the friends of enemies. In Algiers this meant chiefly Colonel Godard, director of security, the last man left there who had been directly involved in 13 May (de Gaulle had done a lot of promoting and deploying since then). He also let go Pierre Guillaumat who, at the Ministry of the Armed Forces, had been keen on concessions and the saving of insurrectionist face. But much more important, Jacques Soustelle – the brightest Gaullist mind, the convert to the Algerian cause from the left, in so many ways the star of the morning – had opposed action against the insurgents, as well he might. He was sacked from the cabinet and set out on the path leading him to last-throw brigandage and disgrace. All of this had been done without parliament, but by way of tying down all corners, parliament was called up to give a huge majority to new (and repressive) legislation demanded by de Gaulle to defend the state and maintain order. In the assembly vote (441 to 75), less than a tenth of the Muslim components, the loyal Harkis, voted against the President and for the *colons* who had provoked it. There were also charges brought against the leaders of the demonstration. De Sérigny was prosecuted as was Lagaillarde, also one Jean-Marie Le Pen.

What remained for the conspirators who had created de Gaulle was no more than the sad fate of men who, having power, extend trust. Four generals, less realistic than Massu who had been an irregular when they were correct official figures, made their essay, a sad and calamitous gesture. The Organization of the Secret Army was created for the purpose of simple terror. It was incapable of taking real power, which politics exclusively concerns. It might well have killed Charles de Gaulle; the attempt at Petit-Clamart, the most serious, came very close. But the measure of the failure of people like General Salan was that in killing de Gaulle they would have gained nothing but emotional satisfaction, a poor basis for political policy. After he had broken the *colons'* power to frighten France, de Gaulle had proceeded by degrees and referenda to the escape route which he had outlined five years earlier to André Philip. The self-determination referendum had taken place in April 1961, with a 'Yes' vote of 75 per cent. No longer caught between two fires, de Gaulle had proceeded after that vote to his fall-back option. He had said to Philip, remember, 'The only outcome is via the independence of Algeria by stages, if possible in association with France.' *If possible*. And since it was not possible, having dispatched his settler enemies, he went within a year to Évian and negotiated with the representative of the FLN the independence of a sovereign Algerian nation.

The generals who had believed in *Algérie française* had re-invented de Gaulle, otherwise a delightful memoirist reflecting in retreat on the folly of government. And the general who did not believe in *Algérie française* abolished it and them. Made by generals, he would turn to the people. (He was strong enough to amend his own constitution through another referendum and make the President no longer the nominee of a college, but one directly elected.) What the people mostly wanted in France was a quiet life, preferably with colonies, but if necessary, without. De Gaulle, perceived as a high nationalist, 'the incarnation of France' as he had delicately put it, disencumbered France of the imperial trophy of 1830 because it was no use to France and destructive of French government. He had understood the *colons* indeed and extended to them, after 1962 and four years of supple manipulation, the full right to return to France.

As for the generals in revolt, they had understood not timing, co-ordination, the need for allies, the Shakespearian injunction about taking one tide, or the stylish and bottomless duplicity of acting Brigadier-General de Gaulle. He understood all these things and very probably connived at their treason, certainly rose by it and lived (despite their late best efforts) to reprieve them after conviction for a very similar sort of treason: one which, not having prospered, could be *called* treason. He had balanced nobles and people (in Machiavelli's sense) so well as to stand very comfortably astride both.

A prophet armed – armed with government, its attendant platforms and publicity outlets and, up to a dithering point, with the actual soldiers of the French army – had triumphed in the way that Machiavelli's prophet armed is supposed to triumph. But he also triumphed because he was a very clever prophet.

CHAPTER SEVEN

How a prince should organize his militia: The
NKVD and the SS compared and contrasted

(*The Prince* XIV)

'A prince therefore must have no other object or thought nor
acquire skill in anything except war, its organization and its
discipline.'

We do not care for Machiavelli's doctrine, set out at the very
beginning of chapter 14 of *The Prince*; and the hard sentiment
it expresses is rendered even less acceptable to modern readers
by the next few words: 'The art of war is all that is expected
of a ruler.' Tell that to the Department of Health or the
Department of Employment. They expect to spend money
exponentially; they also expect to be blamed for what they do
not accomplish. But whatever better things we aspire to, a
cold truth attaches to his central argument: 'There is simply no
comparison between a man who is armed and one who is not.
It is unreasonable to expect that an armed man should obey
one who is not.'

Machiavelli has in mind those who, acquiring force, become
rulers. He speaks of Francesco Sforza who 'because he was
armed, from being an ordinary citizen, rose to be Duke of
Milan.' Being armed, for Sforza, meant commanding an effective body of soldiers.

The notion is one entirely apt for this century. Armed men
have risen to be more than Duke of Milan. But the phrase
which Machiavelli uses in this chapter to describe the force

which arms take, 'militia', is even more pertinent. For though some men, like General Franco, have risen through the use of regular troops, it is the militias, the private armies, the troops pledged to a man and/or an idea, which concern us here. Take the Nazi film *The Triumph of the Will*, a noisily overpraised work which impresses me only as tedious, repetitive propaganda. Nevertheless it tells you something. Hitler, its star, doesn't merely rant, he assembles his regiments of blond adoring young men. They call out in choreographed form the cities they come from, represent and murder you for: 'Bremen', 'Augsburg', 'Chemnitz' or 'Magdeburg'. These are Hitler's militia, the Brownshirts or SA, the means by which he armed himself for his struggle *before* he actually enjoyed power.

In the film he goes along a line of new formations attended by a standard-bearer carrying a flag which had done service in the Munich putsch. With proper religious form he touches each new flag with the old, an odd echo of the service of laying-on of hands, a touching for transmitted magic. This, though, was the Devil's own apostolicism.

Some of the SA regiments are comic, not least the young heavies of the agricultural corps who actually shoulder spades to march. Others, like the brand-new SS in their black uniforms – here led by a fussy, little cuff-shooting football referee of a man, Heinrich Himmler – are not. But these are militias all right. They did not seize power for Hitler, but without them it is not easy to see him having reached it.

The purpose of bodies of armed men among civilians is ambiguous; that purpose havers between intimidation and seduction. Orwell has a remark about the goose-step which applies to these marching men: 'It says "I am ridiculous, but you dare not laugh at me."' An English builder who visited Germany twenty-five years earlier, in 1910, said on his return, 'There will be a war all right. It isn't just that the kids there play soldiers, they drill.' Those words of my own grandfather bring an English perspective to things: that however much we may like scarlet jackets and bandsmen, too much soldiering is neither natural nor right.

This is the old English horror of a standing army, the English belief that the military are slightly disreputable and that such activities should be left to the odd people who enjoy them. Kipling of course disagreed, but Kipling was at least brushed by Fascism. Orwell again speaks of troopers as 'farm labourers and slum proletarians officered by a specialized sub-group of the upper class'. The idea of all of us ardently joining in, dressing up and marching about is as absurd and off-colour as that of turning our eyes in synchronized rapture upon a single leader-cum-redeemer.

The Triumph of the Will is tosh, but instructive tosh. It is wrapped in mystique, another thing the English don't have much time for. It shows soldiering as a sort of redemption. The saddest thing about it is the expression of pathetic, innocent devotion on the faces of those young men, bright- and wide-eyed and evidently believing in the goodness of what they are doing. It speaks the sexy charm of violence (especially violence tensed, waiting and on show, dress-violence as it were), but it also illustrates the innocence, the trusting faith of the means, which is to say of the young men. They are assembled for a purpose which is uncomplicatedly evil. In a little over ten years' time they will have very nigh conquered a continent and then lost it in a war of twenty million dead among whom they will lie in great numbers. It is awesome but it is also rather good politics.

The Germans, at the time of Hitler's ascent to power, suffered from two things: humiliation born of defeat followed by a punitive peace, and a militaristic tradition going back to the early eighteenth century when King Frederick William of Prussia kept soldiers like a stamp collection. The exaltation of the soldier as the elect of the earth, not as a poor squaddy with no better luck than to get stuffed into a uniform, had and has fearful potential. Hitler did not offer his Brownshirts as a way of actually seizing power. He had had a hard lesson in the Munich putsch and had learned it very well. There would be no paramilitary snatch at power. Instead he offered show, swagger, ersatz soldiering, street theatre and something which people who were *not* soldiers could belong to in imitation of the real thing. It was a club most people could join, but the very Jewish observation of Groucho Marx about that sort of thing would have been quite lost on the wide-eyed young men.

The militia may have reached its baleful high point in the storm-troops of Hitler, a high point to be marked with a grave cairn in the doings of another militia, Himmler's SS – not an army but something out of the Book of the Revelation. But the route to this summit was marked with many earlier and blessedly lesser forces. If there was a root of the modern private army, it was surely the Freikorps. These are touched upon in the account of Ernst Röhm and his unacceptable counterbalancing powers as head of the SA under Hitler. But the SA was a confluence of many former Freikorps activists that occurred at the return of crisis in 1930–1. The Freikorps proper flourished from the end of the First World War until they were discredited by their own excesses, including the murder of Rathenau, the Kapp putsch and Hitler's own Munich fling in 1923, and made redundant by the return of economic prosperity and political stability at about the same time.

These bands had been created in the first place as an immediate response to the mutinies and left-wing risings which affected the German navy and army in the last days of the war. When Admiral von Hipper's ships refused orders to leave harbour, Kiel, Bremen and Cuxhaven quickly became areas of revolt which, through the eyes of militarism, looked like miniature soviets. And would-be soviets of workers' committees did spring up across Germany. The failure of war turned swiftly into a challenge to both civilian government and to military authority. The example of the Bolshevik revolution was one year old and the government in Berlin was desperate to restore authority.

That government was supposedly Liberal and Social Democratic, but there are few quarrels like those dividing the same creed. Lenin had spoken in his pointed way of supporting the Social Democrats as the rope supports the hanged man, and Gustav Noske, once a basket-weaver in Brandenburg, now a pillar of the SDP and a major force in the post-war government, understood the simile in the spirit in which it was intended. He would later put that showy phrase into practice against the far left. But in Kiel he ended the mutiny by persuasion, a tour de force of political skill. But this localized mutiny, headed by a relatively moderate sailors' committee, spread to factories and cities across Germany where the parties of the far left – the Independent Social Democrats (USPD), followed later by the newly formed Communists (KPD) – made themselves felt. When they did so – most notably with the Spartacist rising that paralysed Berlin (an enterprise in which the insurgents had the full co-operation of a political police chief, Emil Eichhorn) – the provisional government, with Noske, now Minister of Defence, as its driving force, took the defence of order and the status quo as their brief.

Their main instrument and in effect the father of the Freikorps was, ironically, the most creditable, disciplined and moderate exemplar, General Ludwig von Märcker. But apart from not being a freebooter or an extreme right-wing reactionary, what distinguished von Märcker was his grasp of opportunity. Disaster, military humiliation, revolutionary activity and the prospect of a degrading peace which would deprive Germany of a significant legal army, all tended to encourage what he wanted: 'A vast militia of bourgeoisie and peasants grouped round the flag for the re-establishment of order'. The near-echo of Machiavelli, the raiser of militias, is audible even though Florence was not exposed to the Leninist instincts of its workers (the *chiompi* lacked that sort of heightened consciousness). The notion of salvation by a militia from the external enemies who traduced the city republic is at the heart of Machiavelli's here-and-now preoccupations. Von Märcker's Freikorps was in his tradition. In the language of its own constitution, this Freikorps was strictly voluntary, existed to keep order within the nation and to defend its frontiers, and it had the category of *Vertreuensmann* (Hitler was to be one of these, a sort of superior NCO liaising with officers). Un-Italianly, it treated pillage as a capital offence and tended to exalt the honour of the ordinary soldier, a response to the then-current spirit of mutiny against traditional over-discipline.

What mattered most about the Freikorps in their early days is that they were effective. Von Märcker himself was directly involved in the military assault on Berlin and the putting-down of the Spartacists. The Freikorps would restore conventional order in other places, Bremen, Halle, Munich with its soviet, among them. And von Märcker's loyal troops would go to Weimar, the city of Goethe and Schiller. After the advance guard had been overpowered and taken prisoner by the local armed leftists, the main contingent surrounded and finally took the future home of the national assembly. It was like sending an irregular corps to take Oxford from the local reds before setting up parliament there.

But although von Märcker, a senior officer and military moderate, worked happily with the SDP and Catholic Centre coalition, which both sought the final defeat of Spartacism and benefited from the first democratic elections, the Freikorps, always splintered into scores of different bands, was something altogether more and worse than the rough irregular means to this respectable end. Von Märcker was no more representative than Peter von Heydebreck, head of a band called the Werewolves: 'I will not forget these days of criminals . . . the days of the revolution will for ever be a blight on German history. As the scum hate me I remain strong. The day will yet come when I will knock the truth into these people and tear the mask from the faces of the whole miserable, pathetic lot.' Heydebreck's words were not aimed at the Spartacists or the KPD or at Rosa Luxemburg and Karl Liebknecht (who had been murdered by a Freikorps group under a certain Captain Pabst), but at the 'November criminals', the members of the centre–left government who had called the Freikorps into existence and who, with the highest military men deserting responsibility and command, had signed peace terms in circumstances created by the defeat of the highest military men.

The militia conceived of by Machiavelli was both exalted and functional. It would serve the nation, the city–state, or even the united Italy of his mental doodle. Machiavelli did not, however, imagine a militia that embodied an *alternative* Florence or Italy, a parallel to government and a threat to it. The bands of Freikorps represented something different from simple reaction, though in the light of their actions one might be excused the confusion. They were the products of the intense nationalism of the pre-war years but also of the contempt of sons for fathers, born of the Nietzschean cult of the hero and of a dozen mystical adolescent discontents. The spirit was remote from the British soldiers' song:

> *I don't want to join the army*
> *I don't want to go to war*
> *I want to stay at home*
> *Living on the earnings of a whore*

The British equivalent of the Freikorps volunteer did exist and he found a niche in life either as a colonist in places like Rhodesia or as an irregular soldier in Ireland – a Black and Tan – an occupation with altogether less merit than living on the wages of a whore. There would be ex-soldiers in the ranks of British Fascism, first under Arnold Leese then Mosley, but British Fascism remained a contradiction in terms; the single serious encounter, at Cable Street in the East End, was a rebuff for the marching men. And even the Baldwin government, limp in so many respects, summoned the energy to pass the Public Order Act of 1936 which outlawed paramilitary parades and the wearing of uniforms, a piece of modest legislation which tersely sufficed.

Militias of a Fascist sort proliferated in Europe from the twenties onward, the original Fascists in Italy, of course, and various imitators: the Belgian Rexists, the Irish Blueshirts, the monstrous Hungarian Arrow Cross and Romanian Iron Guard and, perhaps worst of all, the Croatian Uštaše, illegal in unified Yugoslavia, whose slaughter of Serbs in 1941–2 staggered the Nazis themselves before Mussolini stopped it. There were British-style fiascos in Scandinavia. But in Austria, both a native corps, the Stahlhelm, run by the many-scutcheoned aristocrat, von Starhemberg, and a pro-Nazi group had the sort of substantial backing natural to that not entirely charming country.

The actual word 'militia' or '*milice*' would not recur until the German conquest of France, when the petty *ligues* of the French ultra-right would provide manpower for intimidatory groups working sweetly with the German command and SS. It was to be the glory of the *milice* to have played a central role in the deportation of Jews to what awaited them in the east, the Vichy authorities showing a protectiveness to Jews of native French extraction and a happy readiness to let *foreign* Jews go their way to the bonfire.

The *ligues* were an older phenomenon than anything in Italy or Germany. France had a tradition of an irreconcilable right, full of military yearnings and exhalations, whose super-patriot-ism was doomed by splendid and finished irony to find fulfil-ment in treason. The organizations of the twenties and the thirties, like the Croix-de-Fer of Colonel de La Roque and the followers of men like Déat and Doriot, had antecedents back in the last decades of the nineteenth century. The anti-Dreyfusards were certainly given to shows of public strength, and their politics – nationalist, nativist, anti-Semitic, patriotic-mystical, French-Wagnerian, had most of the ingredients of what we loosely call Fascism. (They and their successors, especially the Action Française of Charles Maurras, were substantially nastier than anything Mussolini would ever offer.) The entire episode of General Georges Boulanger, the flimsy military totem who seemed poised in 1886 to seize power by *coup de main*, but flinched and killed himself, turned upon the use of regular troops. But then perhaps the true significance of the private armies of the third and fourth decades of our melancholy century has been the recognition by less tentative Boulangers that one may, as it were, roll one's own.

The right wing armed groups shared Machiavelli's predicament. He was casting around for means either to protect Florence or make Italy; they for means to impress many people, the legal government of the day, their left-wing opponents, themselves. I have spoken so far exclusively in terms of the Fascist or French pre-Fascist right as employers of militia. But for all their love of parody-soldiering, the right did not have exclusive use of the civilian drilled as soldier. In Ireland a force did arise which would claim the name of militia. The Irish Republican Brotherhood, subsequently the Irish Republican Army (with immediate precursors in Fenianism and some would say an earlier tradition of Whiteboys and Ribbonmen), burst upon the general public consciousness with the Easter rising of 1916 and the seizing of the Dublin General Post Office, also with the parallel but less halo-encircled attempt to land German arms in County Kerry.

The Brotherhood sought by violent means to obtain the whole of what boring constitutional politics under the Irish Parliamentary Party's leaders, notably John Redmond, had achieved a part – national independence as against an undertaking for Home Rule at the end of the war. The most publicized figure in the movement, Padraig Pearse, a bad poet on emotional horseback, believed in what he sweetly called 'blood sacrifice'. 'We may,' said this murderous windbag, 'make mistakes in the beginning and shoot the wrong people; but bloodshed is a cleansing and sanctifying thing.' It could be the century speaking.

He was joined, among others, by James Connolly, socialist, internationalist, and in every particular a superior article. It was said of Connolly (by Eoin MacNeill) that 'he had a notion that once a stand was made, however brief in Dublin, the country would turn in a mass against the British government and overthrow it'.

So it roughly and readily proved. The armed struggle of the IRA, ignited by the rising and fuelled by the imbecile executions of fifteen participants, did not defeat the British in any military sense. The attempt could have been put down. But the fighting, a series of skirmishes, armed raids and random shootings of policemen and soldiers, produced two simultaneous British reactions. One was the blockheaded, enraged desire of officers in the field to take reprisals: the shooting into a crowd at a football match in November 1920 in response to a mass IRA killing is the classic example of growing your own new enemies. The other reaction found expression in the liberal, legally scrupulous British tradition which turned away with increasing disgust from involvement in this sort of bloody mess.

It is also true that events before the rising – the acceptance of Home Rule as a principle, the growing concentration of Unionist energies upon secure separate status for most of Ulster – made the treaty of 1922 very much less of a sacrifice for London than it would have been ten years earlier. To Lloyd George it was a matter of face and of a curious reverse-Leninism: 'We have murder by the throat,' he declared before taking it, in the person of Arthur Griffith, by the hand.

What Connolly in his less exalted moments had dismissed as 'our physical force friends' had existed before in Ireland, and the IRA exists today, from time to time killing a nurse with Semtex at a memorial service *pour encourager les autres*. But it would dwindle quickly to the margins; and it was an IRA man, Éamon De Valera who, despite his fussing omnipresence in the new state, became the custodian of an Irish Republic not easy to distinguish as a society from the dominion John Redmond had sought.

The IRA was the creation of rhetoric and, in return, itself created splendid theatre. The Civil War following the Anglo-Irish war was bloodier and the rule of the Free State much harsher than its predecessor. The new Justice Minister, O'Higgins, executed many times more IRA men than the British military governor and did so to widespread Irish approval. As an irregular militia, the IRB/IRA can claim to have detonated something. But its chief claim is upon mythology. The British left the twenty-six counties of Ireland irked, exasperated and embarrassed when, after foolish delays, they had at last planned an orderly withdrawal. For a militia to achieve a *coup de style* is interesting; but *useful*?

Machiavelli might dream but he dealt in realities, and the entire sequence of events in 1916, as recounted after 1918, might best be seen not as the making of history but the garlanding of it.

Ironically, the most successful militia of all in terms of effect-to-numbers ratio, though also nationalist, belongs, if anywhere, on the left of politics, certainly to the annals of respectable liberal history. The shirts of coercive street politics – black, brown, grey, blue or whatever, so admirably parodied by P. G. Wodehouse in the black *shorts* of Roderick Spode's outfit – owe at least a sartorial debt to a man who, despite despotic twitches, would have aimed his rifle at them, Giuseppe Garibaldi.

Given the subsequent history of the political shirt, it may only seem apt that Garibaldi should have bought the distinctive uniform of the Thousand cut-price from suppliers to the Buenos Aires slaughterhouses. But the Thousand themselves fully realized Machiavelli's dream: 'Before all else it is essential to raise a citizen army; for there can be no more loyal more true or better troops' . . . and as for the man who would lead such a force . . . 'What doors would be closed to him? What people would deny him their obedience? What enemy would stand in his way? What Italian would deny him allegiance?' The prophecy was exactly fulfilled in 1860–1 in months and with little blood, and not by an alternative despot like the murderous Cesare Borgia to whom Machiavelli addressed *The Prince*, but by a sentimental, idealistic leftist from Liguria. Italy was united, the Kingdom of Naples overthrown and the Pope left to maunder and anathematize in his Renaissance bunker, by an excitable, arm-waving romantic with a deep vein of generous decency and no end of a flair for irregular soldiering. Machiavelli's injunction had been heeded 350 years on. Sardinian royalty got in on the act and so in every Italian city a Corso Vittorio Emanuele meets a Via Garibaldi. But Christopher Hibbert puts it well:

> The sight of the glittering uniforms, the swaying plumes and helmets had attracted all the peasants of the neighbourhood who gathered round Garibaldi to cheer him. He pulled in his horse and held it back a few paces behind the King's and shouted at the excited people clamouring round him as he pointed to the figure in front, 'This is Vittorio Emanuele, the King, your King, the King of Italy. Viva il Re.' The peasants stared at him uncomprehendingly and, after a moment's silence, burst out again, 'Viva, Viva, Garibaldo.'

What Italian indeed would deny him allegiance?

The fact that the left could command a militia was not lost on the Marxists who came to power in Russia in 1917. Not for nothing did Isaac Deutscher entitle the three volumes of his life of Trotsky *The Prophet Armed*, *The Prophet Unarmed* and *The Prophet Outcast*. 'It is unreasonable to expect that an armed man should obey one who is unarmed, or that an unarmed man should remain safe and secure when his servants are armed.'

It is no accident, a phrase that *Pravda* would immortalize, that the quarrel between Stalin and Trotsky should have begun in respect of the command of troops. Trotsky, made Commissar for War, had pragmatically put former Tsarist officers into important positions (doubled with political commissars to keep them in line), because they were technically trained and liable otherwise to serve somebody else, like the White general, Anton Denikin. It was necessary and agreed to by Lenin, but not popular and there was considerable opposition which Stalin, Commissar for Nationalities and active in the north Caucasus, exploited in every possible way. The original view of the party had been to replace the army with a people's militia, but with 40,000 former officers and 200,000 ex-NCOs on hand it was foolish not to use them (under surveillance).

Stalin, in the name of pure doctrine, defied Trotsky and assembled in his territory a group of politically reliable henchmen with modest military backgrounds. The key men were Klimenti Voroshilov, Sergo Ordzhonikidze and Semyon Budenny, all of whom would rise as Stalin rose. Voroshilov, on Stalin's recommendation, was made commander of the Tenth Army, something for which he, an oilfield union agitator, was ludicrously under-qualified. A message sent by Stalin to Lenin at this time is quite eloquent:

> For the good of the cause I must have military powers . . . but I have received no reply. Very well. In that event I myself, without formalities, will remove the army commanders and commissars who are ruining things. That's what the interests of the cause bid me do, and naturally, the absence of a piece of paper from Trotsky won't stop me.

This was tolerated but when Stalin redoubled his efforts and encouraged local commanders to ignore the orders of Trotsky's War Council (effectively the Ministry of Defence) and himself countermanded the orders of General Sytin, Southern Front commander and Trotsky's official appointment, Trotsky responded very reasonably by demanding and getting Stalin's dismissal and threatening Voroshilov with a court-martial. Stalin was recalled, but honourably and with membership of two key committees of government. The implications were ferocious. Trotsky was the creator of the Red Army, the winner of the Civil War, a sort of genius. But he was a follower of Marx rather than Machiavelli, a genuine soldier, but also a Jewish intellectual with the makings, at the hands of his followers, of a posthumous world bore. The idea that it is unreasonable that an armed man should obey one who is unarmed would have struck him as banal. So it is, so banal that Stalin, a man of inferior mind and glinting purpose, understood it.

As it happens, Stalin's grasp of the essence of power was accompanied by the sort of grudge that is useful in the entrenching of victory and the burying of opponents in the entrenchment, but can also be grievously overdone. An important part of the great purge which Stalin, nearly two decades on, as godlike, all-powerful ruler, imposed on his country, was an assault on the high command of the Red Army. The chief victim in this group was Mikhail Tukhachevsky, the principal commander in the field during the Polish War, a genuine hero, not to say People's Hero, who had been preoccupied since the war with making the Red Army technically proficient and up-to-date. He was Trotsky's appointment and, having been gazetted second lieutenant in the Semeonovsky Guards in 1914, was a former Tsarist officer.

The prosecution of Tukhachevsky and, with him, army commanders Yakir and Uborevich, Kork the head of the Frunze Military Academy and Gamarnik, First Deputy Commissar for Defence since 1923 (who would commit suicide), was originally based upon the evidence of another officer, the Trotskyist Dmitri Schmidt, beaten and tortured into deposition. But it turned chiefly upon a document fed by the NKVD, Stalin's secret police, to the SS who, through a coming man, Reinhard

Heydrich, passed it around governments on tolerable terms with the USSR, like those of Czechoslovakia and France, before gracefully returning it to the NKVD.

The process, over two major trials in 1937 and 1938, killed off (literally) 3 out of 5 Soviet marshals, 13 out of 15 army commanders, 8 out of 9 admirals grade 1, 50 out of 57 corps commanders and 154 out of 186 divisional commanders. Such a cull of the professional soldiery certainly ensured instant deference to the central government, but the advance of the Wehrmacht to the Black Sea and Moscow and mile-high losses were the price paid; as were the amenability of Stalin to the proposals brought by Ribbentrop in 1939 and Stalin's own immediate unwillingness to believe in the invasion of 1941 when it happened. The miracle was that a Zhukov and a Koniev could still be found to combine with the private heroism of young soldiers to reverse Stalin's own home-made calamity. The negative military usefulness of Marshals Voroshilov and Budenny, commanders in early stages of the war, merely underlines all distinctions between the political and the military.

Ordzhonikidze did *not* live to command in the war. One of the few humanly decent men near the top in Stalin's regime and given to arguing back, he responded to the arrest of his deputy, Pyatakov, with outrage and a clear understanding that it presaged his own downfall. 'Comrade Sergo, look what they're saying about you' had been Stalin's message accompanying the confessions of tortured prisoners. Having at least upbraided Stalin on the telephone, Ordzhonikidze shot himself, was reported by four doctors as having had a heart attack. Stalin being nothing if not thorough, the four doctors were then themselves shot. But both the other north Caucasian chums survived as cronies; Voroshilov, a man of magical amenability, and very much Keitel to Stalin's Hitler, became state president and had a city named after him. Irony brought the Nazis to the gates of another renamed city, Stalingrad, thus the site of a triumph which Stalin himself would appropriate, but formerly Tsaritsyn where his quarrels with Trotsky, just concluded with an ice-pick in Mexico, had long ago begun.

In forming a fighting force to protect the state by exercise of the art of war (Machiavelli's terms), Trotsky out-performed Stalin a hundredfold. The army which he created – extensively from Tsarist military ranks – would one day save the Soviet Union in spite of Stalin. But a militia in our time has only in a secondary sense, or through an offshoot like the Waffen SS, been a fighting force. We are quickly back with *The Triumph of the Will*, with a militia whose purpose is one of policing and strengthening the political base through terror. In the pursuit of this, Stalin was without peer. The Cheka, created by Feliks Dzerzhinsky at the outset of the revolution, was one thing and not nice, but it was to be vastly improved upon, first under the name OGPU then as the NKVD. Dmitri Schmidt, as a follower of Trotsky, could in 1927 wave his dress sword at Stalin, roundly abuse him and threaten one day to cut his ears off. Ten years later, just for old times' sake and as an aid to research into the crimes of Trotsky's generals, he would be tortured into saying anything and then shot.

The death of Dzerzhinsky's successor Menzhinsky, like him a Pole, would be used some time later to confect a plot against his successor, Yagoda. And the assassination of Stalin's effective deputy Kirov, almost certainly on Stalin's orders, was followed by a wave of enough repressive legislation to persuade retired and smouldering brigadiers that Christmas had come all year round: capital punishment for unauthorized leaving of the country, capital punishment available at the age of twelve, family of man in flight liable to twenty years in jail if they knew of it and five if they didn't. Then came successive waves of arrests by the NKVD: old Bolsheviks, the high command, doctors, and as a mark of its own standing as a mature power within the state, officers of the NKVD. Of twenty NKVD commissars listed officially in November 1935, every single one – apart from one murdered without forms of law – was, sooner or later, arrested and shot as an enemy of the people, which God knows they were.

It was of course in the purest Machiavellian spirit of employing over-zealous lieutenants that successively renamed secret police forces – the Cheka, OGPU, MVD and NKVD before the benign, playful KGB of our own times – served to take the blame for what Stalin had bidden them to do. The Christlike secret policeman '*qui tollit peccata mundi*', who bears all blame, is a charming concept and was operated cheerfully as Yagoda died for the death of Menzhinsky, and Yezhov for 'excesses' – otherwise the crimes of Stalin. Coupled with the huge cult of the leader, expressed in a thousand pictorial images of him sucking on his Dunhill pipe like a Caucasian Stanley Baldwin, the terrible but sacrificial policeman conjured up, as Alan Bullock puts it, the old phrase, 'if only the Little Father knew'. For the citizen to blame the NKVD was dangerous but only human. It could be done at any rate silently, *in pectore*, but the proof of success of Stalin's rule was the extent to which, even after his death and Khrushchev's secret speech to the twentieth congress of the party, Stalin was *not* blamed.

The Soviet secret police were a militia incomparable but for the one obvious comparison. They had their own command structure, uniform and all the accoutrements of an army, this assembly of firing-squads with gold frogging. They held the armed forces themselves in subordination, a subordination based in wise fear. They supervised arrests, torturings, trials; through the hands of Stalin's creatures, like the judge, Ulrikh, they were engaged in the prosecution, killing and imprisonment of many millions. They entered the lives of people like trolls or thought-forms. The tale of Pavlik Mrozov, to whom statues long stood, and who was killed by uncles after denouncing his own father – an example of and to Soviet youth – speaks the penetration and acceptance of the police mode into Soviet lore. Though subordinate to Stalin, this militia had equality (at the low col which lay below the peak of the leader himself) with the party. In a system which spoke of the 'leading role of the party' this was high enough.

And yet they existed to conceal Stalin's own power. In a grisly way, they were the executive branch. They were terror. But having so much power, they never seized it all. Though the greatest compliment paid to them was that of Stalin's immediate collective succession who, having lived through the last terror, moved to have Beria and the Minister for State Security, Abakumov, arrested, tried and shot, in so far as such things could be distinguished in the world this militia had made.

Making distinctions between the secret policemen of the USSR and Nazi Germany themselves recalls Samuel Johnson's observation about granting precedence between a louse and a flea. But the differences are interesting. Hitler, the aborted artist and architect, succeeded, with some help from a woman director in political cinema, in the choreography of a big chorus-line. His storm-troops were (partly) for show and they have continued to exercise a fascination for cinema directors ever since. However much the Nazi characters in war films are identified as evil, they invariably fascinate the director. There is a Scarpia-fascination about the filmic Nazi officer; the intellectuals wittering on about Leni Riefenstahl concede more than they know.

Stalin, though served by better directors (and ones just as servile) had no artistic purpose. *His* secret policemen were functional; they took you away and killed you. The NKVD had a great measure of power, but it wasn't on show and anyway it lacked the dress sense of the SS. The two militias reflected the princes they served. Hitler was an orator, an electric presence, a fascinator who advanced by dazzling and throwing handfuls of destiny in people's eyes. Stalin was a bureaucrat, an office politician, a man who would have risen irresistibly within the BBC (or IBM or the Hanson organization, though Gordon White's admiration was for the Nazi). He lacked style and force in public speech; his addresses on film sound like any bored minister of state reading a brief, and quite lack the zing of John

Gummer. Stalin was as terrible a man as has ever lived, but in the way not of Bluebeard but of the quiet suburban multiple murderer. And Stalin, oddly for disorganized Russia, was the man of system.

However staged and lit, a death's a death, for all that. But one final distinction must be made. The Soviet policemen were different from the SA (far more terrible) and from the SS (less specific). To be a Jew under Hitler and the SS *was* death; to be anybody at all under Stalin and the NKVD *might* be death. Faced by such unimaginable doings, the last word should go to Orwell who understood such things:

> It happened that Jessie and Bluebell had both whelped soon after the hay harvest, giving birth between them to nine sturdy puppies. As soon as they were weaned, Napoleon took them away from their mothers saying that he would make himself responsible for their education. He took them up into a loft which could only be reached by a ladder from the harness room, and there kept them in such seclusion that the rest of the farm soon forgot their existence . . . [and a little later] . . .
>
> Napoleon stood up and casting a peculiar sidelong glance at Snowball, uttered a high-pitched whimper of a kind no one had ever heard him utter before.
>
> At this there was a terrible baying sound outside, and nine enormous dogs wearing brass-studded collars came bounding into the barn. They dashed straight for Snowball who only sprang from his place just in time to escape their snapping jaws. In a moment he was out of the door and they were after him . . . they were the puppies Napoleon had taken away from their mothers and reared privately. Though not yet full-grown, they were huge dogs and as fierce-looking as wolves. They kept close to Napoleon. It was noticed that they wagged their tails to him in the same way as the other dogs had been used to do to Mr Jones.

CHAPTER EIGHT

Generosity and parsimony; Cruelty and compassion:
Thoughts in passing on Kennedy and
Khrushchev, but, chiefly, the expensive,
effective career of Juan Domingo Perón

(*The Prince* XVI and XVII)

If there is any passage in *The Prince* which is lightly and airily
quoted, especially by people who have not read *The Prince*, it is
the one about whether it is better to be loved or feared. 'The
answer is one would like to be both the one and the other; but
because it is difficult to combine them, it is far better to be feared
than loved if you cannot be both.' It has a nice hard ring to it and
fits with facile daily assumptions about toughness. But has it
actually been true in our time? Stalin managed to be super-
abundantly feared, though usefully at one remove through his
apostolic vicars, the NKVD; he was also loved in a way which
Machiavelli would have approved – by humble people for
perceived greatness. Vladimir Nabokov, who loathed Stalin, has
a White Russian colonel of exemplary non-socialist inclinations
praising the new tsar, the Tsar Josef. Stalin is admired yet, not
only in his native Georgia, but among older people and among
the most nationalistic. Cruelty, the *res dura* (harsh necessity) of
Virgil whom Machiavelli at his stuffiest, most *Times* leader-like,
approvingly quotes, is excused where it is not actually applauded
by all those for whom national grandeur counts most. The

Hungarians taking such a pride in their fifth-century connections still give the name Attila.

But the curse of generalization, for which Machiavelli has a sweeping taste, is of not being true all the time. And at the end of Stalin's ministrations, a way had to be found out of the terror. The men who succeeded Stalin would never commit crimes like his or get the respect he was freely given. In this exact sense Machiavelli was right. They were seen as mediocrities. Nikita Khrushchev in particular was disliked for his crude peasant manners, as displayed when he banged his shoe on the desk at the United Nations General Assembly. But Khrushchev, grievously inculpated as a servant of Stalin in the Ukraine before the war, was right in his changes of national conduct. He simply had, after 1953, to bring terror to an end. His own part had been played during a game of terrified leapfrog when a line of men made backs for successors and for their own submission and death.

Khrushchev did end the terror, replacing it with a repression which, excepting only the events of Hungary in 1956, was modest and very nearly bloodless. Men who had assuredly not conspired against Stalin had been tortured, tried and shot, and with them their remotest relations, friends and fleeting acquaintance. Those who *did* conspire against Khrushchev, the 'anti-party group' of Zhukov, Molotov, Malenkov, Shepilov and others, were demoted to boring jobs – in Malenkov's case, to management of a power-station nearer to Nanking than Moscow. But they were not killed. Khrushchev won some love, but the echoing street comment on him was one of disgruntlement with his lack of greatness, greatness as Fielding understood it in his praise of Jonathan Wild, of overarching and grandiose criminality. He had set aside systemic atrocity but he was dreadfully common.

Yet Khrushchev was right. Crime did have to stop, even if the useful commodity of fear became, in the process, a banked capital to be gradually used up. The sixteenth century, though a hard place, peopled with its Borgias, della Roveres and Tudors, thought of fear in exemplary, not epidemic terms. The cool assumptions of Machiavelli about means and ends clinically considered, which led to so many pulpit and tract denunciations of the man, can still be rationally entered into. That Hitler should kill Gregor Strasser and Captain Röhm, and Stalin kill Bukharin, Zinoviev and Trotsky, constitutes the working requirement of raw political force; but the carpets of death laid end to end by the two neighbour regimes between roughly 1935 and 1945 defy dispassion. The twentieth century has seen broad-screen annihilation: the Western Front, the Hitler camps and the Stalin camps, and deaths in such millions as no insouciance can take in its stride.

What one wants is an ounce of civet to sweeten the imagination. It comes perhaps if with Machiavelli chapter 17 (fear and gratitude) we couple Machiavelli chapter 16 and the closely allied question of whether a prince should be generous or parsimonious. The arguments are of course related: do you try to please or not and will not the pleaser end in the classic Florentine judgement by whoring after goodwill and not finding it? Samuel Johnson informed Lord Chesterfield that he had found the love of great men to be a native of the rocks. Machiavelli thought as much of the people's love. In chapter 17 he says:

> One can make this generalization about men, they are fickle, liars and deceivers, they shun danger and are greedy for profit; while you treat them well they are yours. They would shed their blood for you, risk their property, their lives, so long, as I said above, as danger is remote; but when you are in danger they turn against you.

The scorn of great men and those who do their thinking for them for the low natures of the poor multitude whom great men intend to use, is instructive. It is echoed in our man's treatment of generosity:

If you do in fact earn a reputation for generosity, you will come to grief. This is because if your generosity is good and sincere, it may pass unnoticed and it will not save you from being reproached for its opposite. If you want to acquire a reputation for generosity, therefore, you have to be ostentatiously lavish; and a prince acting in that fashion will soon squander all his resources, only to be forced in the end, if he wants to maintain his reputation, to lay excessive burdens on the people, to impose extortionate taxes and to do everything else he can to raise money. Thus he will start to make his subjects hate him and since he will have impoverished himself, he will be generally despised.

There is so much here that could be quoted with approval by Conservative Central Office. And certainly the experience of socialist parties has been that the balance of advantage between the gratitude (or love) of those benefited and the resentment of those taxed is, to put it mildly, uncertain. And the argument all turns on similar considerations to those in Machiavelli's love and fear chapter. The public are a low lot who can't be relied on to give value for a bribe. Machiavelli also throws in the useful observation: 'Whatever you do, don't spend your own money.' One is tempted to stop and argue with him here, using the instance of John Fitzgerald Kennedy, idol and icon to the age, who spent a phenomenal amount of his own money, or his father's, and to great account.

In casual accounts of Kennedy one thing hardly ever discussed is the use of money during the 1960 primary campaign, particularly in the states of Wisconsin and West Virginia, in order for him to perform well against Hubert Humphrey. It isn't unimportant that Humphrey, a politician with an activist record, a busy, hard-working liberal senator, a crusading, early-in-the-day advocate of total racial integration, who had written what were then called 'negro rights' into the Democratic platform as early as 1948, had an incomparable merit claim over

Kennedy, a poolside legislator with no record of social concern and a mighty apathy on the race issue. But Kennedy and his family threw money into the primaries as if it were going to be withdrawn from circulation. The poor Protestant state of West Virginia, which had to prove that it could elect a Catholic, received money for advertising and general expenditure in amounts – just within the law – which should have guaranteed popular appeal to the candidacy of the better sort of Satanist. One can argue about the lines dividing advertising and distribution of funds. But certainly expenditure in such circumstances of one's own money (if one has enough of it, and the Kennedys assuredly did) can be splendidly effective. American government, good and bad, has commonly lived by such expenditure.

Broadly, however, sensible men in power will always want to spend other people's money. Government is wonderfully adapted to it. A man who spent public funds with gusto and style and whose example is delightfully instructive was Juan Domingo Perón, President of Argentina, significantly in this context *three times* elected President of Argentina!

Argentina is a country with elements of tragedy. An editor of one of its major papers once told me that the reason Argentina made such enormous noise about its patriotism – the perpetual excited claim to the islands (Falklands to the British, Malvinas to Argentinians) – was because it had no patriots. The upper classes were Europeans first and last, spending most of the year in Europe, while the Italian immigrants used the phrase *a fare Argentina*, 'doing Argentina' (though in truth enough of them stayed: Argentina has a large Italian population). The middle class also looked to Europe, especially Britain, the old proprietor, and led a national self-contempt. The workers had no corporate understanding and had produced the most destructive and short-sighted union movement on earth. No wonder, having so few roots, said the editor, that Argentinians made such play of their patriotism, no wonder they went to shout in the Plaza de Mayo for '*Malvinas argentinas*', investing in these mudflats with thermal springs feelings they expected of themselves.

It is also a country deeply stratified: between classes, between races and between the cities – supremely Buenos Aires, a delectable city – and the back country. Harsh names described their country poor: *cabecitas negras, pelos duros* – black heads, hard hides. All these attitudes would come together when the unions organized on behalf of Juan Perón a massive influx of the poor, *criollo* (part-Indian) and country people to that beautiful city. A phrase used at the time sticks eloquently in the mind: *una deluga zoológica*.

The country had been governed with harshness by either Manchester School liberals or generals of the army. An attempt at recognizable European radical and democratic government, undertaken by Hipólito Yrigoyen, had been ended by a coup in 1930. There had always been extensive electoral fraud, largely on the part of the proprietor right. The powers of landowners, expressed through the Sociedad Rural, were, in a country with slender manufactures, enormously weighty. And the poor were very poor. The population of the capital had grown fast as a result of migration from the countryside and from overseas (it doubled to 800,000 in the eight years before 1943), and unions were small – 60,000 members in all. In circumstances of vast inert wage-push, what might be called wage-lean, there was a vacuum with no one equipped to push.

Yet the man who supplied the push, and in so doing did indeed spend other people's money and thereby tested the Machiavellian guidelines, was at first sight a singularly improbable candidate. Juan Domingo Perón came from a middle-class professional background, though his father had reverted to the land to become a farmer of merino sheep. He himself had rejected his grandfather's profession of medicine for study at the military academy. Despite a mediocre start half-way down his class, he went on to an excellent conventional career with something of an academic bent, writing a number of books, mostly strategic-historical, but one of them on the place-names of the hinterland. He was, after all, a *criollo*.

However, he held conventional middle-class conservative opinions. As a young officer in 1930, he travelled into the city as a rank-and-file executant of the military coup which overthrew Yrigoyen for his infamous left-democratic practices. In his earliest days he had been army fencing champion and a good boxer, but also a leader whose batman observed that his shopping-trips for Lieutenant Perón had mostly been for books. He moved steadily up the military ranks and took the opportunity afforded for travel, not least to Italy (where he met and admired Mussolini), to Spain during the Civil War, Portugal under that pious male Thatcher, the dismal Salazar, Yugoslavia and Albania. Under the post-1930 military regime, he had increased responsibilities and his personal reputation and influence grew inside the army.

In the process he became something of an admirer of Adolf Hitler and German National Socialism. This fact would naturally be much used against Perón by his enemies when he came to power. The United States, happy in its associations with the Somoza family in Nicaragua, with Stroessner in Paraguay and Trujillo in the Dominican Republic, *inter* so many *alia*, made enormous righteous capital of this, as did *La Prensa*, the Anglophile Manchester School press outlet for both free speech and the inheriting class.

Perón was to organize no gas chambers and conduct no massacres. When anti-Semitism was trumpeted by elements among his supporters in his first election, he flatly disowned them – and an exploitable Jewish community did exist in Buenos Aires. Without lingering too long on the fine points of ideology, it would be best to see Perón, apart from the elements of pure opportunism, as one of those people who admired Hitler for doing things, for fast-moving social action, autobahn-building, unemployment-cutting and the general flexing of the muscles of splendid young men. Perón was not averse to physical bullying and street roughnecking, he was also a fervent anti-Communist; but whatever his rhetoric, he never approached the killing habits of civilized Europe, western or eastern. He had absorbed the doctrines of the Strasser brothers rather than of Hitler himself, and he would discover a great talent for that mysterious and lamentable thing, 'charisma' (he was to be a dab hand on a balcony).

He was a Fascist of sorts, not least in his corporate economics, in the street force used by his heavies and in his utilization of physical numbers, also in his intolerance of the voices of contradiction, notably anti-Peronist newspapers like *La Prensa* and *La Nación*. His relationship with democracy had less to do with belief in it than of being good at it, of having the useful ability to win elections in rough coincidence with its rules. An Argentinian politician, a former foreign minister with whom I once discussed the topic of Peronism, said that there was no European equivalent for this odd mixture of populism, socialism, Fascism, syndicalism, on-and-off clerical elements and nationalism. 'Except,' he said after a pause, 'except possibly for Fíanna Fáil!'

The truly interesting side of Perón, however, and why he should interest a student of Machiavelli, is that more than most politicians, he did (with other people's money) a great deal for the most poor and, having done it, he retained the love – there is no other word for it – of great numbers of the poorest people until his death. The Argentinian novelist Ernesto Sábato writes of the coup that ousted Peron:

That night of September 1955, while we doctors, landowners and writers were noisily celebrating the downfall of the tyrant in the living-room, in a corner of the kitchen I noticed that the two Indian girls who worked there had their eyes full of tears. And although during all those years I had meditated on the tragic dualism which divided the Argentinian people, it struck me most movingly . . . Great multitudes of humble

[146]

fellow countrymen were symbolized by those two Indian girls weeping in a kitchen in Salta.

Yet he came to his first share of power in a routine right-wing military coup, staged in 1943, as one of the shadow junta of four. It was the latest in a series since the new constitutional politics of Yrigoyen had been bundled out by General Juan-Felix Uriburu in 1930. (Significantly Yrigoyen also retained support after his fall, something demonstrated in local elections unwisely called by the general.) Behind the 1943 coup stood the four colonels, Ávalos, González, Ramírez and Perón. The generals involved, by contrast, were lay figures conferring dignity and holding presidential office at the direction of the colonels. Military government was not enough for the new men, who fancied themselves as something even more depressing.

The colonels headed GOU, Grupo Obra de Unificación – Group for the Work of Unification. Their serious ambition was to unify not Argentina, but South America. Proceeding first by way of client nations like Paraguay and Bolivia, then through supposedly sympathetic states like Chile, Argentina would fulfil a manifest destiny as the leader of a unified South America against the domination of the United States. Such bullfrogging ambition had its epitaph in the observation of Gabriel García Márquez, who is a Colombian, that 'We South Americans all have an Argentinian inside us, alas'. The colonels observed European unification taking place. 'The greatest and best-equipped nation must rule the destinies of the newly formed continent . . . In Europe that nation will be Germany.' In the same tedious and comic-unpleasant document, the colonels made two other observations: 'In our days Germany has given life a heroic meaning' and 'Hitler's struggle in war and peace shall be our guide.' (The document containing these statements was furiously denied and called a forgery, but Eduardo Crawley, the helpful historian of Argentina, finds it in key with

[147]

the acknowledged statements of the military clique and says that 'if it was a forgery, it was an exceedingly good one'.)

Most things in South America come late. An attempt at paralleling Nazi Germany after El Alamein and spot on time for the Badoglio coup in Italy represented an excruciating timing, as comic as it was disagreeable. The curse of Argentina was imitation of Europe. *La Prensa* – still run in 1987, when I called there, from offices like Brooks's Club – followed the English; Yrigoyen had looked to French radicalism. The colonels looked to Hitler.

The document also contains one of those steel-stomached remarks which go as much with sado-monetarism as Spanish-colonial replica Nazism: 'An iron-hard dictatorship was necessary to impose on the people the renunciations this formidable programme called for . . . The people shall be attracted, but they will inevitably have to work, suffer deprivations and obey.'

The irony of Perón's career was that at a certain point he threw clean out of the window the notion of the people being given a hard time and told that it was good for them. Like shrewd politicians before him, he sought out an unfashionable, unwanted job, the distinctly junior Department of Labour. Unions in Argentina had been knocked about and kept in their place during the preceding thirteen years of conservative rule. And the colonels were of course worse. They responded to the provocative existence of unions by arresting their leaders and exiling them to Patagonia, Argentina's half-hearted answer to Siberia.

But Perón listened to the arguments of a Spanish statistician, José Figuerola, with political experience as a minister in the Primo de Rivera government in his native country. There Figuerola had set up corporate-style industrial arbitration boards. He also understood the wretched condition of manual workers. He pointed out that socialists and communists took most credit with the workers but, as the losing side in politics, had little to show by way of concrete achievements. All they could offer was attitudinizing rhetoric.

Perón listened hard and responded. Innocuously he followed the early suggestions by the colonels that unions should join government-sponsored committees, but demonstrated his good faith by organizing the release of one prominent union leader and making a major wage concession (40 per cent). Perón set about making the government's tame union front vividly attractive to workers in terms of their own interests, but no longer tame. If it was a honey trap, it was sticky with delights. He also developed a line of rhetoric that was distinctly anti-capitalist: 'We must not forget that in our territory there are men who used to earn 20 centavos a day; not a few who earned 12 pesos a month; and not a few either who earned 30 pesos a month . . . Nowadays we have – and blessed be God, may it continue for many years – industrialists who can make profits of 1,000 per cent.'

Fascists had abused capitalism before and made appeals to labour. Perón went further than anyone else had and would, when fully in power, proceed to extensive redistribution. Words, though he was extremely good with them, were only words, but the money jingled. There had been settled bases for power in Argentina: the middle classes, land and capital, the armed forces – but never labour. Labour was affiliated to parties vetoed by the other interests, and indeed Perón's rhetoric was not untrue. The crushing subordination of labour had, as in England a hundred years before, proved very comfortable for business. Perón had recognized a gap in the political market. He was also placed to do something that none of the men on horseback or in armoured cars had ever done: make the army and an army regime actually popular with great numbers of the people. Under the influence of Figuerola, he was opting for a soft Fascism, one which sought to please and which, by delivering goods, services and a rising living-standard to the worst-off, outflanked the left and put the right in the unpromising position of calling for more poverty. It was not good economics, but it was wonderful politics.

Perón had not yet, as Labour Minister then Secretary, done all of this, but he was bidding fair to; and when opponents outside and within the junta sought to make an end of his power, he would demonstrate another political strength, a flair for publicity and public oration which those opponents could have done without. Meanwhile, during 1944, he used his position as Labour Secretary with powers of decree to shift boots on to other feet, signing in that year two hundred agreements between employers and unions, bringing in paid holidays, starting the regulation of rural working conditions and setting up labour tribunals. The institutions mattered as much as the money. The phrase 'dignity of labour' may be hackneyed, but the yearning for it exists, not least in countries where labour has been despised and excluded. Beer and sandwiches at 10 Downing Street are an aspect of status and a source of vicarious self-respect. An independent labour-law specialist, Ernesto Krotoschin, compared the changes made, 'a sudden sweeping-away of certain obstacles to the development of the working masses, both in the political and juridical fields', with the changes which in 1936 had taken place in France under Léon Blum!

Politically, Colonel Perón could deliver to his colleagues in the shadow junta, perturbed as they were that the German horse they were backing had shot himself, something concrete achieved, whether or not they liked it: their official labour federation which had been scorned initially but was now accepted by workers, and a new access of popular support. He moved up to what had been thought the key job in government, Secretary for War, but prudently took his Labour Department with him. The other colonels and the members of the official government were not so naïve as to miss the point that the real access of support was for Colonel Perón. Having also cut an active and impressive figure organizing relief for the victims of an earthquake in the province of San Juan, Perón looked, as the saying goes, 'unassailable' and was made Vice-President with every prospect of the succession. At the same time he had inevitably made dangerous enemies among the establishment of Argentinian money and 'society', not to mention the United States, never fastidious about involvement in the internal affairs of any country, which roundly denounced him.

The United States, in its deep understanding of diplomacy, restraint and good form, sent to Buenos Aires as ambassador one Spruille Braden, Mr Roosevelt's nuncio to the backward, who was described as thinking that Providence had given him the mission of destroying the regime in Argentina, something he sought to do by encouraging business in that country to confront the government.

The confrontation involved the old opponents of the regime – parliamentary legitimists and socialists, even Communists – as well as the business community. Braden organized a demonstration *marcha de la constitución y la libertad*. Since larger grievances than those of the employers and the Americans were involved, the numbers were high. Perón, though, as minister in charge of higher wages, limited hours and strong union power was the immediate practical target of those most intimately involved. Rocked by the demonstration and under general pressure, the men of iron in the junta began to melt. In fact, once Perón had been seen to get ahead of the rest of the military, ordinary rivalry served to make compliance with outside pressure very acceptable to sections of the government. Given the handle of a peccadillo of the most South American sort on Perón's part (the obtaining of a job for Uncle Oscar, his mistress's mother's lover), the leading member of the junta and commander of the garrison, General (no longer Colonel) Ávalos required Perón's resignation.

The latter's reaction demonstrated that in the workers to whom he had given wages, legal protection and self-respect, he had a priceless asset; that though nervous, he knew how to exploit that asset, and that as a piazza orator he was hot politics. Humbly submitting and giving up all his offices, he begged only a last farewell meeting with his people, the workers. Granting it was common good manners and elementary error. There had been nothing like that encounter since Irving's last farewell. And it proved every bit as elastic. The membership were informed by the unions and bussed into town until the square holding the ministry not far from the presidential palace was overflowing with very solid numbers, if not yet from the zoological deluge referred to earlier. Perón not only took leave of his friends, the workers, he suggested that his sacking could be followed by the loss of the wages and rights he had brought and he announced his last decree, a further wage increase coupled with a national minimum index-linked salary.

That and the suggestion that his dismissal was the consequence of the decree said everything that was necessary. The government was now merrily screwed between two sets of pressure, capital plus respectable politics plus the United States against the workers who, unlike the other three, could and did go on strike.

Perón then went to an island in the delta having told his colleagues that he was going to the hills inland. In the time spent trying to find him in the wrong place, the next workers' demonstration – pro-Perón and anti-the rest of the regime – took place and ended with bullets flying and demonstrators dead: bad politics even for men in epaulettes who fancy their own ferrous natures. Not very intelligently, the flustered regime arrested Perón. Even worse, they put him on the same island which had held Yrigoyen; very sensibly his close colleague Colonel Domingo Mercante set about getting out the workers. (Perón's wife, the ambiguous Eva, would, at a subsequent date, ghost-write herself up, quite spuriously, as the heroine of the occasion.) Perón himself gracefully pointed out that he was ill (genuinely – with pleurisy), that he was detained without charges and that he requested these charges to be openly brought.

With demonstrations taking place and the labour federation voting for a general strike, the government made its next mistake by bringing Perón back to Buenos Aires. Much better to have tenderly and solicitously transferred him in protective custody to some healthy spot in the hills a thousand miles from the capital. The time elapsed had allowed the unions and Colonel Mercante to get properly organized and to come into Buenos Aires in the sort of dismaying numbers with which governments do not care to argue. The black heads and hard hides, the rude mechanicals, the organized meat-packers, labourers in from the country, all made their way down to the city. General Ávalos had put up the swing-bridge; they used bridges upstream and commandeered boats, some even swam.

It was such a crowd as the police does not fire upon. Though the naval commander, Hector Vernengo Lima, was ready to; a counter-coup was contemplated by his faction in the government. But after negotiations with Mercante, the cabinet agreed on a compromise by which there would be reconciliation, with Perón sharply unarrested, though he would not return to the government; but his friends would, and Perón would concentrate on the serious business of running for President in the upcoming, more or less free, elections.

One calls it a compromise, but the speech which Perón was allowed to make – last government mistake of the episode – though lamentably soupy stuff, glittered with menace and said very plainly whose boot had kicked for him and whom it might yet kick. It also sucked up to the workers treating them as half-interest and half-sacrament:

I leave the honourable and sacred uniform the Fatherland gave me to put on the civilian's jacket and blend into this suffering sweating mass whose work makes the greatness of the Fatherland . . .

[153]

I want to take this opportunity, as a mere civilian, of blending into this sweating mass, of embracing it with all my heart as I would with my mother . . . Day by day we shall incorporate to this beautiful mass's movement each of the hapless or discontented so that, together with us, they too shall become a beautiful, patriotic mass like you.

And perhaps most important, certainly in the context of Machiavelli: 'Many times they told me that this people for whom I had sacrificed my hours of my days and nights would betray me. May those unworthy dissemblers know that the people does not deceive those who help it.'

In fact, for all the glutinous excess of Perón's prose style, what he was saying was true. He had delivered to the workers, the workers had understood and had responded with a whole-hearted mass assertion of their political existence. Everyone was too polite to say so, but the government had been overthrown. As Eduardo Crawley puts it:

An unusual revolution had taken place. A government had been overthrown, not by the Army or by the threat of armed action, but by the mass mobilization of workers whose only strength was their sheer physical presence and their fervour. And when the anti-Peronisto Admiral Vernengo Lima tried to take the High Seas Fleet into rebellion, the fleet politely declined.

Machiavelli's scorn for the people – and the black heads and hard skins were assuredly the people – is hardly sustainable in the circumstances: 'ungrateful, fickle, liars and deceivers . . . they would shed their blood for you as long, as I said above, danger is remote'. This crowd, familiar with a recent bout of shooting and killing, walked through police cordons with no knowledge that they would stay inactive. Again, whatever Perón's early motives, something like a genuine bond had grown between him and the workers.

Here was a military man, a supposed Fascist who had thought roseate things about Hitler, who had yet persuaded hard-driven workers to unite as a massive political force as no European socialist party, and indeed no communist party, had done. The French and Italian CPs had their 'manifestations', of course, and some of their influence in the late forties and early fifties derived indirectly from government apprehension at the numbers of demonstrators involved. But they did not bring a government down and indeed they never came to any government as the disagreeable surprise which Perón laid on in the Plaza de Mayo. Lenin himself, though he benefited from a mutiny, employed groups of shock troops which made the 1917 revolution more like a putsch than the will of the working people.

The consequences were long-lasting. Perón (ably helped again by United States Ambassador Braden, by now US Under-Secretary for Foreign Affairs, and for the moment playing interim-buddies with the Roman Catholic hierarchy), was elected President the next year, 1946, with 55 per cent of the votes cast, together with absolute majorities in both the legislature and the upper house.

His slogan was *Perón cumple* (Perón fulfils) and on the whole he did. Whether such fulfilment was for the long-term good of Argentina is another matter. Economic wisdom comes in the West German style with the workers able, through sophisticated and expertly advised unions, to treat the economy as an equity and behave with at least as much perspicacity as stockholders about investmentworthiness, unit production costs and the strength of the currency. Argentinian workers were kept swiftly and immediately sweet with inflationary consequences which a later finance minister of that country described as requiring every Argentinian taxi-driver to keep three sets of figures for the currency in his head at the same time. But hospitals, a nationalized railway system and telephone network, some cheap rearmament from war stock being sold off, the steady building of schools and low-cost housing, pension schemes extracted as social cost from employers, were nothing if not a decisive policy, nothing if not fulfilment.

The Perón government gained an additional dimension from the personality of the President's wife, the former Maria Eva Duarte. An actress and radio singer who, like her mother and sisters, set about advancement by sleeping with the right men, Maria Eva would graduate to the fate worse than all other fates, death included, of being set to music by Andrew Lloyd Webber. In the show's hit song she urged Argentina not to cry for her. She was roundly accused by the conventional conservative press of having close Nazi affiliations and of helping a prominent German to leave the country. The probability is that Evita, as she winsomely liked to be called, only slept with the winning side and soon grew wise to the prospects of Germany winning. But via a Colonel Imbert, head of posts and radio who, on gratification, was able to get her into the Argentinian equivalent of films, namely assured parts in radio plays and serials, she graduated to be the mistress and later the wife of Perón, who was able to get her into power.

In Machiavelli's day, a woman like Eva might perfectly well have had influence, but not in the brittle, theatrical and noisy form which it took in her case. But then one of the few essential differences between his time and ours is the role, not so much of women as of publicity. Florence in its immortal days had no consultants in public relations. What Eva thought about anything is almost bottomlessly unimportant; what she was seen to do and be was real politics. Excluded by a snobbish ladies' charitable circle from the customary patronage vested in the President's wife, Eva set up her own foundation which swiftly left the official body nowhere. The money for it was raised by both legal and dubious means, including state extortion and an element of genteel protection as well as honest contributions from the unions and many little ones from ordinary people.

Legal or illegal, there was a lot of money and it was handed out with maximum publicity. One probably does best to think of the Blessed Eva as any contemporary lady-on-TV – a heart bleeding on camera who never did badly out of doing good. The Fundación Eva Perón was never subjected to audit; its ventures and expenditure were capricious, including a mischievous contribution for 'the needy children of Washington'. But the core of its work, represented by twelve hospitals, hostels for girls at work, inexpensive public housing, old people's homes, cheap grocery stores and 160 schools, represented something to poor and working people – something which usually had the name 'Perón' prominently written up outside over the lintel in large letters.

Peronism frequently looked much more left-wing than right. With its mixture of charity and gangsterism, it belonged very much in a Catholic society. Accountancy, after all, is very much a Protestant and Jewish profession. The phrase 'Bias to the poor' comes to mind, but it was a bias made to work by graft, audit amnesty, and legal accommodation of the fund by the Congress so as to give it all the tax advantages of a charity and all the independence of a private company.

The comparison with Fíanna Fáil is not casual. Irish politics, both in Ireland and the United States, was long marked by the rise of corrupt but popular politicians who oiled wheels and set in train great engines of irregular public benevolence. The pork-barrel itself was once more literal than metaphorical, represented by the Christmas basket of groceries. The church hierarchy's horror of socialism but cool view of capitalism and helpful concept of venial sin, the willingness of business to buy itself favours from politicians or politicians for favours, the practice of street enforcement and small-time thuggery are all very much at one with Perón's practice. A recent reviewer of a life of James Michael Curley, the twice-jailed, four-times-elected Mayor of Boston, actually quotes a phrase current in Perón's Argentina to measure his man: 'Before Perón I was poor and I was nobody. Now I am only poor.'

Sub specie aeter–itatis Eva Perón does not matter. She was a woman of some character and courage and no taste at all who may have meant well, but who also meant to cut a figure and enjoy celebrity. She did genuinely useful things in an irregular, sometimes corrupt, way with the usefulness outrunning the wrongdoing. But Eva paralleled and massively strengthened the basic political purpose of her husband. She identified with the bottom of the heap, did primary-coloured good to them as a sort of larcenous Lady Bountiful, and made exactly his political sartorial appeal. He had told the workers that he was putting off his officer's uniform, forsaking his right of promotion to general (in fact he duly took the extra star without blushing and putting on the jacket of the ordinary worker). Eva said that her people were the *descamisados*, the shirtless ones. It is not the private love-affairs of Eva's early life which are embarrassing but the platonic and elevated public ones with the poor, the workers and 'her people'.

It might be vulgar and naff, it might be shot through with cheap and factitious sentimentality and personal advantage-seeking. It was accompanied by the minor brutalities of minor Fascism. There is everything to be said for leaving the redistribution of wealth to someone like Clement Attlee who will have thought of 'charisma' as something done by Edmundo Ros. Protestant rectitude can usually raise social standards without screwing up the whole economy. But when Eva died, which she did very early (of leukaemia), she was fiercely loved; and the poor in their innocent way did not merely turn out in huge, plangent numbers, they erected (with natural help from the government) a cult – again very Catholic though not blessed by the hierarchy – of instant sanctity: pictures of Evita bathed in celestial light, prayerettes beginning 'Hail Maria Eva'. In a country with a tradition of treating women very badly, the cult confected its own alternative Queen of Heaven. For a sexpot who slept her way up, a peddler of political influence and fixer of jobs like Uncle Oscar's appointment at Posts and Telegraphs, a buddy of some sort to Nazi embassy officials and a practitioner of oceanic kitsch, she had come a long way.

The significance of Eva is that she did all the things discouraged and warned against by Machiavelli – though she took his point about not spending her own money, and she almost certainly (if only carelessly) enriched herself – but she created a force of sympathy, gratitude, affection, a sort of *schwärmerei* for the Peróns which outlived her and outlives him. Perón himself was re-elected. After expulsion by another coup of rather pure-minded generals led by the very different, upright and naturally never popular Eduardo Lonardi, after a mighty quarrel with the church and unpleasant charges about his private life, he would come back to power yet again in the 1970s (with an imitation Eva, the unmeritable Isabelita). The very government in power at the moment of writing, that of Carlos Menem, is expressly Peronist, sustained by support from the Peronist party, though in all conscience it is not very Peronist in its vigorous anti-inflationary practice.

Since the advent of Perón, Argentina has moved from a position of serious aspirant to major-nation status to that of economic invalid, has known 1000 per cent inflation, relays of civilian and military governments, extensive urban terrorism followed by a military counter-terror embraced with bloodthirsty delight by the middle classes, and has made and lost war for the desolate Falklands which have joined Eva Perón as a national cult. Argentina has been almost endemically ill-governed. But Peronism has lasted fifty years since spending its first public money to make friends. Machiavelli's point carries in terms of good government, but it hardly holds in the face of self-interest ruinously triumphant in Argentina.

CHAPTER NINE

How princes should honour their word: The frugal gratitude of General Francisco Franco

(*The Prince* XVIII)

Machiavelli utters in this chapter his famous dictum of the lion and the fox. A lion is defenceless against traps and a fox defenceless against wolves. A prince must then be a fox to recognize traps and a lion to frighten off wolves. 'So it follows,' he says in a famous passage, 'that a prudent ruler cannot, and must not, honour his word when it places him at a disadvantage and when the reasons for which he made his promise no longer exist.' He later mentions a ruler 'whom it is better not to name' (identified in a footnote as Ferdinand of Aragon) who 'never preaches anything except peace and good faith and is an enemy of both one and the other, and if he had ever honoured either of them he would have lost either his standing or his state many times over'.

Francisco Franco, Caudillo and Captain–General of Spain, who made much play of being a plain bluff soldier (always a sign of baroque political sophistication), may or may not have made a study of Machiavelli; but he had no need to. Like King Ferdinand, Franco would *say* anything. Ironically, his left–wing opponents have been able to paint him as the blackest of Nazi sympathizers on the strength only of words – in praise of Hitler, of totalitarianism, of anything: words uttered to soothe people of that unpleasant sort whom he then signally failed to accommodate in any practical way. Having achieved power with German and (even more) with Italian support by March 1939, he was confronted very early with the calling-in of debts when the Second World War followed within six months.

When that war was declared between Germany and the British–French alliance on 3 September, Spain declared strict neutrality on the 4th. On 12 July 1940, after Mussolini, Franco's particular benefactor, had come into the war, this became non-belligerency – a diplomatic euphemism for being unevenly even-handed, more neutral towards one side than the other. On 17 July 1941 Franco stated: 'The destruction of communism, the terrible nightmare of our generation, is now absolutely inevitable. The Allies made a mistake when they declared war and they have lost it.' On 14 February 1942 he praised Germany as 'the defender of European civilization', adding that 'if ever the road to Berlin were open, then not merely one division of Spanish volunteers, but a million Spaniards would go there to bar the way'. In 1942 Franco mobilized troops in Morocco in response to the gathering of Allied transports at Gibraltar. When American and British forces invaded French Africa, those troops stood still. In 1943 Franco again returned Spain to neutrality.

Franco's obligation to Hitler was substantial. The Condor Legion had fought for him, arms had been readily supplied to offset the Russian arms of his opponents (who were helped less by Russian military advice). More to the point, Hitler's Germany was the dominant power in western Europe for the first four years of Franco's rule in Spain. Even more to the point, Germany looked like the winning side. There were traps of several sorts with honey enough in them. But Franco, despite his verbal contribution to the German cause, demonstrated a systematic chastity not occasioned by innocence.

He was early pressed by the Führer to make common cause, and on 23 October 1940 the two men met at Hendaye in the Pyrenees, a meeting for which Franco was, deliberately, an hour late. The gesture was emblematic. 'I'll have to use every trick I can – and this is one of them. If I make Hitler wait, he will be at a psychological disadvantage from the start.' The objective for Hitler and the purpose of the meeting was the facilitation of Operation Felix which had replaced Operation Sealion, the direct, cross-Channel, P&O invasion of Britain. Operation Felix, which aimed at domination of the western end of the Mediterranean and the barring of the British from North Africa, involved German air bases in Spain and Spanish co-operation across the straits in Morocco. It would also involve twenty divisions attacking Gibraltar by land. Gibraltar would fall on 10 January 1941 said Hitler, for whom prophecy had been understating performance lately. It would be handed to Spain and there would likely be some colonial *petit cadeau* as well.

No Englishman understands the significance of Gibraltar to the Spanish, a promontory of their own land-mass in foreign hands since 1713. For any ruler of Spain to spurn restitution of this psychological jewel requires astonishing fortitude. But Franco's energies were bent upon inventing excuses for not receiving the rock from German hands. Spain was impoverished and hungry at the end of the Civil War; could Germany supply it all, a hundred and ten million quintals (one million tons) of grain perhaps? Hitler could only offer a hundred thousand (waiting in Lisbon, if Franco accommodated him). Dearly as Spain cherished Gibraltar, explained the General, she must win it for herself; acceptance from the hands of an ally offended touchy points of Spanish pride. But actual Spanish conquest would require sophisticated heavy weaponry . . . and time. Could Germany supply the weapons? Also training in their use: would the Germans provide *that* over a further period of anxious time?

These were difficulties raised by a man who wants difficulties to save him from assent, the old-fashioned girl's insistence that she has to wash her hair. But Franco also entered quiet caveats against Hitler's military plans. The British were to be driven out of Africa. They might, said Franco, be driven to the edge of the desert, but behind that, they could fall back on their colonies in central Africa, and central Africa would be protected against major attacks by the desert belt in the same way that an island is protected by the open sea. 'As an old African campaigner, I am certain of that.' As for twenty German divisions crossing Spain to attack Gibraltar, did the Führer perhaps not appreciate the awful nature of the Spanish roads and the winter weather with its mud in the valleys and ice in the hill country? Franco's gently and diffidently presented mixture of requests, excuses and technical difficulties had the effect, remarkable in such company, of making Hitler 'feel like a Jew'. He also remarked that he would as lief have three teeth out as spend another day with the Spaniard.

The Hendaye meeting produced a secret protocol: Spanish entry into the war without a date, African territories for Spain, but not identified, a sort of trading of nothing for nothing between high contracting parties. When the German Foreign Minister, Ribbentrop, left the final protocol–drafting session with his opposite number, he told his interpreter that Franco was a coward without gratitude and that poor Serrano, the Spanish Foreign Minister and Franco's brother-in-law, pro-German but doing as bidden, was a Jesuit. Yet even as he rescued the sweets of the trap, Franco snatched something from it without penalty. Given British preoccupation and German desire to court Spain, he felt safe to denounce the internationalization agreement on Tangier, taking that city as a Spanish possession: a small chicken for a careful fox, spoils for a spectator practising self-help.

Franco's problems with his prospective allies were paralleled by divisions at home. He was a military conqueror, but he acted in the name of the broad conservative forces of church, army and middle class, almost indeed a popular front. This was a grouping which it would be inaccurate to call 'Fascist' *tout court*. There existed as a form of Fascism the Falange, a party with a uniformed militia aspiring to parallel the army and be an integral estate of the nation. Here, amongst its leadership, headed by the same Ramon Serrano Suñer, were found the consistent advocates of a German alliance; and Serrano, having accompanied Franco to the meeting at Hendaye, would meet Hitler officially again, but this time alone, at Berchtesgaden.

And yet although in the view of George Hills, his biographer, Franco would all his life applaud and honour the Falange, it never did become an estate of the realm or influence Franco's personal government of Spain. He had not created it, but was painfully indebted to it for its support. The debt was paid in words and empty office, not in a share of serious power. As for Serrano, his function was to be promoted to Foreign Minister at the height of Hitler's domination after the French defeat, in place of Colonel Juan Beigbeder who was friendly to the British. The substitution was made in order to decorate a war-evasion policy with a pro–German holder of office. Effectively, Serrano was a wildfowler's ploy, a bunch of feathers stuck on to a float.

Of the other strands in the national coalition, the church was far from pro-German in outlook, the dying Cardinal Goma – despite having denounced 'the Semitic International' – issuing a pastoral in 1940 stating that Britain and France were fighting to uphold the Christian morality invoked by the Pope. The best of Franco's generals, led by José Varela, now Minister of War, were pro–British in sympathy and Franco privately made himself very clear. After the defeat of France, he said, 'Those people who urge me to go in with Germany are wrong, quite wrong.' He based his belief on a gratifying respect for British military resolution. 'I tell you that the English will never give in. They'll fight and go on fighting; and if they are driven out of Britain, they'll carry on the fight from Canada, they'll get the Americans to come in with them. Germany has not won the war.' Also, as the son of a naval family from the Spanish Portsmouth, El Ferrol, the General stood in genuine awe of the British navy.

The flattery and gross adulation that Franco was to pour on

Hitler by letter and at their meeting are accounted for in the famous Spanish observation that words and feathers are carried away by the wind. His compliment to the British might have weighed as lightly, except that it was not addressed to them and was exactly paralleled by his actual course of action. Something of Franco's settled outlook was contained in his remarks to Marshal Pétain leaving Spain for his fool's destiny as treaty-signer and subsequent head of Vichy France. 'Don't go, Marshal. Make your age an excuse. You, thank God, were here and in no way responsible. Let those who lost the war, sign the peace. You are the hero of Verdun. Don't let your name be mingled with the others who have been defeated.' They are the words of a fox to a sacrificial beast.

Franco's concern with Hitler was to do nothing either out of gratitude or by way of favour-currying which would involve him in war with Hitler's enemies, but never to say so with such clarity as to persuade Hitler to take what was not being given. Hence the Berchtesgaden meeting with Hitler on 18 November 1940, at which Serrano served as Franco's acceptable face in Nazi circles. Hitler intimated that Germany had 186 divisions inactive and ready for deployment and that 'I have decided to attack Gibraltar'. In fact he had not, having been advised by his military technicians against Operation Felix without equivalent action to close the east of the Mediterranean, something that Franco, as both professional soldier and avoider of commitment, had advised him at Hendaye.

At Berchtesgaden Hitler was told again of Spain's willingness and of her unreadiness. The earlier private observation of Franco to Serrano in the presence of three of his leading military men was that 'Spain cannot and must not take part in the war'. Serrano was thus in no position to give Hitler satisfaction. To the mission from Hitler of Admiral Wilhelm Canaris (Madrid, 5 December 1940) Franco repeated Spanish readiness to go to war – and a litany of British naval superiority, Spanish lack of military preparation and Spanish shortage of food. Hitler then sent Franco a letter of mixed mystical exaltation – 'We three men, the Duce, you and I, are linked together by the most implacable force of history . . .' – and quiet menace: 'The world's most tremendous military machine stands ready . . . and the future will show how good and reliable that instrument is.'

At about this time, Franco paid a visit to Bordighera to talk with Mussolini, to whom, wrote that man's son-in-law and Foreign Minister, the future deserter and firing-squad victim Count Ciano, 'is assigned the task of bringing home the Spanish prodigal son'. Franco thoroughly enjoyed this meeting and commented warmly about Mussolini's honesty with him. Mussolini 'was still convinced that Germany would win the war'. But 'he scarcely tried to persuade me to enter the war . . . he had just suffered severe setbacks in Greece.' Franco asked the Italian leader a question electric with relevance: 'Duce, if you could get out of this war, would you?' And he reported the answer: 'He burst out laughing and, throwing his arms into the air, cried out, "You bet your life I would."' The burnt hand confirmed what the cautious hand had wisely supposed.

Spanish troops would serve on the Axis side after the German invasion of the Soviet Union, passionate anti-communism being one of the General's deep convictions. But they went as volunteers and ironically, as Hills points out, paid Spain's 'blood debt' for German Civil-War assistance twenty times over. But this return of thanks was vicarious and, legally and diplomatically, left Spain a non-belligerent.

On the real issue of Spain joining the Axis, Franco had effectively won his struggle. Felix never took place; German troops did not enter Spain by consent or (with the memory of the Peninsular War before them) without it. Franco was now concerned to telegraph goodwill to the Allies. They, for reasons best known to themselves, looked upon the clerical-monetarist dictator of Portugal, Dr Antonio Salazar, as being a better, more liberal, more western thing than Franco. He was nothing of the sort, having disgraced and degraded the diplomat Sousa Mendes for sitting through three days and nights to provide Jewish refugees in France with visas, something that Franco personally authorized on behalf of Spain. But if the Allies approved of Salazar, it did no harm to be seen talking to him, though Serrano warned it would upset the Germans. A meeting took place on 13 February 1942, deftly ahead of a time when upsetting the Germans would be of no account. There was talk of a neutral Iberian bloc, and although Franco (from the Galician north-west) addressed his neighbour in a frontier dialect that the Portuguese had trouble understanding, the point of the meeting was that it should have taken place and been seen taking place.

The achievement of Franco was to have treated words and reputation with indifference. The (outstandingly stupid) British Ambassador Samuel Hoare was convinced that Franco was pro-Axis and that he, Hoare, had kept him out of the conflict. Hitler was flattered direct; Serrano, an overt Fascist, held ostensible office, the Falangist element was permitted to abuse the British in its newspapers. But the message 'Spain cannot and must not take part in the war' was given when Germany was at its zenith, the obvious winning side. The pressure on Spain to join was very great. It was not yielded to, and when the time came for conspiracy against Franco late in 1941, it came from elements ardent for Germany and close to the German Ambassador.

The war ended in 1945 and the Nazi regime with it. When Franco died it was thirty years later, as Caudillo and Captain-General of Spain, a fox in office.

CHAPTER TEN

The need to avoid contempt and hatred: How
Benito Mussolini was loved until he was hated

(*The Prince* XIX)

Machiavelli's chapter 19 is an estimate of the need of a ruler to
avoid contempt and hatred. Mussolini died before an irregular
firing-squad of his enemies and soon after was hanging upside-
down at the end of a rope in the Piazzale Loreto in Milan. He was
then the object of a well-nigh universal hatred and contempt. But
his life had been expended in the elaborate avoidance of both.

Until almost the end he was very good at it. Not only was
Mussolini not hated in Italy – by all reliable accounts he was
enormously popular. He was also cited abroad for conspicuous
merit, not least by an enthusiastic Winston Churchill. Luigi
Barzini, who wrote very well about him in *The Italians* and had
often, as a young reporter on the *Corriere della Sera*, been a close
eyewitness, describes him performing in the Langhe district.

> Soon enough, Mussolini was leading a parade of thousands of
> frenzied and gesticulating followers . . . He showed no
> expression on his face except the usual wooden determination.
> Mothers lifted babies high for him to see and possibly to touch,
> as they had done to kings in the Middle Ages. At one point, a
> few nuns came running, their long black veils flying in the
> wind, carrying baskets of freshly picked peaches to offer him.
> He accepted their homage without thanking them, without
> turning his head or smiling, and handed the fruit to his retinue.

Nobody who saw it will ever forget the sight of city squares filled with crowds listening to him; the heads were as close together as tesserae in a mosaic, all eyes turned to one focal point, the balcony or stand from which he was speaking. It was an ominous and frightening sight.

Mussolini finished on the losing side after having kept some shocking company; he is also seen through the lens filter of British and American wartime media simplicities which were not very different from the agitprop view – a demonology without refinement or nuance, in which all Fascists were pretty much equal. Fascism, as described by this Hollywood Manichaeism, was a blob of indeterminate evil threatening 'our boys'. The left, buying at the time, very understandably, the Soviet line about fighting Fascism everywhere, made no distinctions. But of course there are distinctions to be made, huge ones where Mussolini is concerned.

He was no sort of monster. Of all the 'Fascist leaders' in Europe – Pavelić, Antonescu, Franco, Horthy, Tiso, not to mention Hitler – he was by many furlongs the least bloody and most merciful. He certainly caused deaths indirectly through his vainglorious and incompetent wars in Ethiopia, Albania and Greece – not least the likely death of anyone with the rotten luck to be an Italian soldier. But he was not the deliberate killer of anyone. Even Giacomo Matteotti, his celebrated victim, subject of a hundred tracts, appears on the best historical evidence *not* to have been his victim. And there is a memorial to Mussolini's way with opponents of the state in the famous study *Christ Stopped at Eboli*. This account of the ancient, deep-dyed misery of Basilicata, the impoverished instep of Italy, was written there by Carlo Levi, a prominent anti-Fascist whose punishment for wrong thinking was exile in that region. He lived in a house and was confined to a village under the negligent if fussy eye of the local mayor and party secretary, was allowed visitors and permitted to have books and writing materials. It is a splendid book, of its kind a great one, underlining the fact that parts of Italy have been a disgrace to the nation under all regimes.

It was not matched by any description of the difficulties of life in Thuringia, or by any exposition of hard times in the Murmansk region. Interestingly, the first, best works of Solzhenitsyn, detailing his experience of camp life (*First Circle*) and of life in exile immediately after release (*Matryona's Home*), were permitted publication under the rule of Nikita Khrushchev. The balance between Khrushchev and Mussolini as civil rulers is about even, though Khrushchev was an attenuator of despotism while Mussolini was a local pioneer. Both are beneficiaries of any distinctions we can be bothered to make between degrees of tyranny.

Mussolini did not kill his opponents. Nor, for that matter, did he share in the great malignancy preoccupying almost everyone else to whom the blanket and inapt word 'Fascist' is attached. He was not anti-Semitic or otherwise racist. He spoke with irony and exasperation of Hitler's feelings on that topic. He was, however, to be drawn half-heartedly and uneasily into racial barrings, bannings and separatings as he was drawn into the great caravan of Hitler's progress in the late thirties, something beautifully described in the novels of the Ferrarese Jewish writer Giorgio Bassani.

Mussolini may not be excused such actions, but they were quite devoid of the ardour of the natural racial persecutors of eastern Europe (and indeed France). In this he was typically Italian. The Italians are not more benevolent than the rest of us, though they were a good deal more civilized than many of their nominal allies in the last war. But their hatreds are internal. Just possibly there might have been serious takers in Milan for a policy of putting Sicilians into camps, but anti-Semitism was thought absurd and wrong, as it was not in France. And the established record of the Italian army, civil servants and even Fascist officials, in cases where Jews were in their jurisdiction, was profoundly different from that of France which, for all its glories, perpetuated some disgraceful traditions through the

Dreyfus Affair and beyond – traditions which found fulfilment under the occupation in the form of deportations to death.

Mussolini was, then, neither a killer nor a racist. What he was, above everything else, was a showman, a practitioner of what the Italians call *con garbo* – flourish, display. So much of what he did was theatre, but it was theatre directed at establishing the self-esteem of Italians through esteem of their ruler. He was thought of as being right-wing, and the proof of that pudding lies in the enthusiasm with which institutions of ownership and established position acclaimed him: banks, Catholic clergy, the military and business all rallied to the regime. The church, incontestably the single most reactionary body in Italy, which had conducted a seventy-year sulk against the Kingdom of Italy, scattering anathemas like the bad fairy at a long christening, was the chief beneficiary of the Duce's positive efforts, emerging with the Concordat of 1929 which still obtains. Mussolini, ironically, was never any kind of Catholic; he had inherited the historic anticlericalism of northern Italy and the former Papal States, where the memory of misgovernment and of the ways of papal gendarmes was long and not sweet. But part of Mussolini's charm and strength lay in the facility that lack of tedious principle can grant a man to concede more than his predecessors. He was the inheritor of a bitter church-against-state snarl-up, out of which every sensible person, some of whom could be found even in the Vatican, wanted to get. In Pius XI he was dealing with a relatively rational Pope, at any rate by the standards of his predecessor and successor. But Mussolini was intelligently aware that the power of the church over its flock was an impediment to government. The Pope, since 1860, had treated the head of state as a usurper and the head of government as a stranger. Pious Catholics were discouraged from involvement in politics or government and made to shape their lives in accordance with the institutional self-pity of the higher clergy. By the Concordat, Mussolini won Catholic Italy for Fascism but also caused at second hand the readmittance of Catholics to public life.

Whether, in the light of the long catalogue of corruption, *clientismo*, accommodation with the Mafia and American intelligence by which Italian Catholic politics have been distinguished since 1945, this was entirely a good thing, who shall say? But it was a success, which is something else. And in terms of chapter 19 of *The Prince*, the avoidance of hatred and contempt, it was skilled and effective princely behaviour.

For Mussolini, of all the people discussed here, is nearest to Machiavelli *in his personal experience*. As an Italian he had problems which the Florentine would have recognized at once. Machiavelli's dearest friend, the historian Francesco Guicciardini, had, as ambassador to two popes, been obliged to accommodate himself to their unwelcome ambitions. But Machiavelli wrote in chapter 19: 'I conclude therefore that when a prince has the goodwill of the people, he must not worry about conspiracies: but when the people are hostile and regard him with hatred, he must go in fear of everything and everyone.' This is high and representative Machiavelli: very simple, incontestable but not generally practised, and expressed with the laconic purity which creates a classic text. And it describes what Mussolini did right as well as what he did hopelessly wrong. He sought real, on-the-ground popularity, he sought to be loved. In this he differed from the great liberal figures of the sixty years of republicanism which preceded him. With the single exception of Garibaldi who was naturally popular and whose flamboyance, simple roots and rough open ways made for adoration, the makers of Italy had not been populist or popular. Cavour, Ricasoli, Massimo d'Azeglio and the other leaders of republican Italy despised cheap popularity. They resembled in every way the fictional Chevalley de Montezuoli created in *The Leopard* by the fine (and mocking) Sicilian hand of Giuseppe Tomasi, that other prince, the Principe di Lampedusa. Chevalley described the new Italian senate for which he asked the Prince of Salina to accept nomination, as:

the High Chamber of the Kingdom. It is the flower of Italy's politicians picked by the wisdom of the sovereign and will discuss, approve or disapprove the laws proposed by the government for the progress of the country; it functions at the same time as spur and brake; it incites good actions and prevents bad ones . . . you will make us hear the voice of this lovely country which is only now sighting the modern world, with so many wounds to heal, so many just desires to be granted.

That sort of high-mindedness is rather admirable. It exalts liberal assumptions about man being capable of anything given education and freedom. It derives from Montesquieu and Rousseau and from Anglophile rejection of absolutism. And however fashionable it has become on the right to deride and even hate Rousseau, liberal optimism is not to be mocked. As was well remarked by an English writer at the very time Mussolini and worse were getting into their stride, 'What is the alternative? What is the dirty trump card ever up dogma's sleeve, to be slid down and sneaked upon opportunity? It is suppression, tyranny in its final brute word force. Look around Europe today and consider under what masks dogma is not feeling for, or openly shaking this weapon to cow the minds of free men . . .' From the essay 'Tradition and Orthodoxy' (1934), those are the words of Sir Arthur Quiller-Couch responding to T. S. Eliot's observation that society was 'worm-eaten with liberalism'.

It was Mussolini's fortune that he came in at an illiberal hour in a country whose liberal tradition, though real, belonged to a middle- and upper-class (and regional) élite. The deal with the Vatican fitted symmetrically in place. Papal power – direct rule in Lazio, Umbria and Mussolini's own Romagna – had been one aspect of the diffuse and variable despotism to which a united but fragile Italy was heir. Princely absolutisms had been another, from Medici and Sforza princes down to the policeman

[173]

princes of the early to mid-nineteenth century, fussbucketing Ernesto, Prince of Parma or King Bomba (Ferdinand of Naples).

Liberal democracy, the conjuring of the people through legislatures by thoughtful and ice-pure Piedmontese and Florentine gentlemen busy in Turin, and their rough friend from Nice, Giuseppe Garibaldi, was only a single strand of the political tradition, and one not strong enough for the First World War, industrialization, the rise of imperialism or human nature.

Mussolini's kind of politics had been exemplified early on in Francesco Crispi, Redshirt and activist for unification, populist radical and early taker-up of the white man's burden. In which latter guise he had, at the end of the last century, anticipated Mussolini with the first Italian essay at seizing Abyssinia. Such crude nationalism is naturally popular, except with serious people like Giuseppe Verdi who, in his eighties, with the consistency of an old radical, observed that Italians were doing to another people what they had fought to prevent yet others doing to themselves. But generally the prince wishing to avoid hatred and contempt is on to a very good thing if he invades somebody. Though, as Mussolini was to find out, that good thing lasts only as long as success. And when success runs out, then, with perfect timing, the waging of war sweetly generates hatred and contempt.

To this we shall return in respect of Mussolini; but for Crispi the move, which ended in military calamity at Adowa in 1896, proved just as disastrous. Indeed, Crispi, nominally a democrat and anticlerical, provided a sort of detailed trailer for Mussolini, the sort of 'strong man' within the system, who, equestrian or otherwise, kept turning up in late 19th-century Europe: Joseph Chamberlain, Boulanger, assorted unpleasant Spaniards and indeed Kaiser Wilhelm. And in the light of what happened to Crispi at Adowa – a great clattering of Italian troops by the Abyssinians – the decision of Mussolini to jump through the same unpromising hoop irresistibly suggests that twice looks like carelessness. Mussolini 'won' in Abyssinia, as he was bound to, but he began his descent there also.

Mussolini's problem was that he could, almost to perfection, do what was necessary to make his government free of hatred and contempt within the limits of the medium-sized, economically modest though healthily developing country in which he lived and ruled. But trouble began when he went international, and when steady success at presentation, long continuation in office and the untruth which accompanies all the best sycophancy gave him a false measure of Italy's military power.

Actual good government concerns us here no more than it concerned Machiavelli (not that he was flatly against it). But the relative success of the Italian economy in the twenties – owing by the way very little to Mussolini – was less important as a measure of princely wisdom than the Duce's outstanding ability to take the credit for it. A harvest of 64 million quintals against the pre-war 49 million had little or nothing to do with Fascism, an energetic if erratic programme of public works suggested rather more. But both indicated better times, since Italy was growing economically in ways beyond the capacity of governments to injure. And Mussolini's genius was for leaving no credit untaken, no trumpet unsounded and no glory not circling his own twitching and receding brow. It was a happy conjunction and threw up, in the early summer of 1925 when a Fascist government had not yet become a Fascist state, an election which, though not of Scandinavian rectitude, was a fair guide to public opinion. Mussolini and the Fascists had 62 per cent of the vote.

Some of the popularity arose from the helpful turn-up of the trade cycle and post-war recovery. There is also a case to be made that Mussolini's ignorance of economics did him no harm at all at a time when the economics of the day were so wrong. There was no Montague Norman figure to exalt the currency and screw down industry and the employee. Fascism's passion for flashy solutions did, practically speaking, set up knots of activity and public works for which leftish commentators are loath to give it credit. There was, in fact, a measure of solar-plexus Keynesianism about and a useful absence of penny wisdom. Italy, a genuinely growing country, may have benefited from receiving sporadic stimulation rather than bankers' judgement.

Most goodwill, however, flowed from the all-singing, all-dancing act which Mussolini kept going throughout his public career. He was, after all, popular enough even in the depression. He was a genuinely hard worker; but although the lights in his office in the Quirinale would be kept burning until after midnight, Mussolini did not have to be tediously *there* for the message to go out *urbi et orbi* how the great man drove himself for Italy's good. He was the first politician properly to use public relations, but the account was not handled by some sleek consultancy. Mussolini fashioned his own. He turned vanity into a marketed asset. He fancied himself as a sportsman, so pictures of Mussolini playing tennis, on horseback, driving a sports car, flying a plane, were all on show. Even at chess, a game which the Duce did not play, he was pictured winning – an example of Walter Mittyism being put to considerable practical use.

This vagueness as to truth was also turned to account where religion was concerned. For anticlericals there was Mussolini's statement of unbelief, for Catholics there was another view of himself . . . as a Catholic. Again, having a built-in, probably genetic tendency to be overweight, he fought the problem with the obsession of a Californian health loon. Violent physical activity, squash, early-morning Swedish exercises (the jogging of the day) and other embarrassing excesses together with a regime of contempt for the table: spaghetti, brown bread, spinach and grapes accompanied by fruit juice or water and a little wine – all served to project Mussolini as the man above gourmetism and sloth. The Mussolini jaw-angle, jutting up and out, which made foreigners laugh but looked masterful at home, probably owed most to his desire not to show any sort of double chin.

Mussolini had been a journalist before he was a politician. He had been a good one. In his Socialist days *Avanti!* never had such a successful, readership-pulling editor. After his break with the Socialists, *Il Popolo d'Italia* was another brilliant success. Now a great part of government, as distinct from *good* government, is journalism. But it is not the journalism of faithful, dispassionate reporting, news sacred and comment free, all that Protestant Anglo-Saxon jazz. Mussolini was not C. P. Scott. The journalism which he understood concerned the making of inert things interesting, the charming of dull readers, the keeping-up of excitement – boosterism as the Americans understood it – plenty of sport, a little politic sex in the manner of the *Daily Telegraph* being sly, and any amount of noise in the form of tromboning, pectoral-twitching leader-writing on the greatness of the nation and the despicable nullity of its enemies.

As ruler of a nation, Mussolini, in his bawling and abuse, bore a fair resemblance to Mr Pott, editor and proprietor of the *Eatanswill Gazette* in *Pickwick Papers*, with his ringing anathemas against 'our miserable contemporary which will shortly drag its contemptible life to a close'. He was, however, Mr Pott combined with Bennett's Denry Machin, the ingenious youth with wheezes for success through publicity who 'annoyed and then disarmed his elders with pure cheek'.

He was also, before the wretched phrase was invented, what is called a charismatic leader: not just *in* the news but the news itself, a leader who exists not to solve problems or make sense of data, but a man to be loved, a hero, a cinema star – in short, a piece of meritorious vibrancy. The answer to Mussolini in more recent times has been the blank icon of John Fitzgerald Kennedy, a man without Mussolini's drive or activity, but one who photographed much better and who had the same knack of living people's lives for them. For the art of avoiding contempt and hatred has greatly grown in dimension and detailed sophistication since Machiavelli's time. It has changed in ways which may to a degree vitiate his famous dictum about the superior nature of fear to love for a statesman. A Renaissance prince gained little from general affection. His peasants did not underwrite his position with their devotion. But a modern leader, even of the undemocratic sort, benefits from the public's emotional identification with him. This was as true of Hitler and Mussolini as it was of Roosevelt or Kennedy.

The Mussolini act was directed to winning such love. Dressed in black shirt and jodhpurs, looking to the unentranced for all the world like a demented film director, he would stride to the tribune of the despised assembly or on to his balcony. He travelled – and this was an innovation among politicians – all about the country. We were to grow accustomed to the American whistle-stop and the British politician talking to meetings up and down the country. But apart from the aberration of Gladstone's Midlothian campaign, the idea of the political leader as mobile presence is a creation of this century with Mussolini in at the start. In the age before television and its coloured shadows, he was the first to use his image to impose himself as the dominant person of the nation.

His appearances were a conscious spending of some of the mystique of government. Those who had seen were disposed to believe. He would be accompanied in the poorer, more backward regions by a secretary carrying a wallet stuffed with thousand-lire bills – actual cash to hand out, but also a sort of profane sacrament and intimation of the intentions of his government. He would thrust these at the poorest and unhappiest-looking in the peasant crowds. People, especially poor people, in a country with a long way to make, do not have much notion of what government is or can do. They are likely to think of it as remote, magical, punitive, unfriendly or nothing to do with them.

Although Mussolini pulled stern faces and strutted like a clockwork brigadier, he also made love to the people. He went to them, laid on hands, had babies lifted up to be seen by him, hands held out to be touched. He worked, in the twenties and thirties of this democratic century, all the ploys and devices of medieval king and church. He materialized, he offered himself as a species of real presence. He was as unlike the frock-coated, high-minded, surrogate Englishness of Cavour and d'Azeglio as a man very well could be. He worked hard at his politics, but he made it easier for an unsophisticated public.

We laugh at his stiff walk, his hand-on-hip gesture, the alpine jaw and the strutting grandiosity of it all. We have seen Jack Oakey in *The Great Dictator* and our taste has been refined by the image-barbers to appreciate nuances like the crinkly Kennedy smile or the Ashdown pained eyes. We persecute Richard Nixon for his dark shave or John Major for saying 'Oh, yes'. But we are jaded sophisticates trained on forty years of the small screen. And Mussolini, as Luigi Barzini said, was like a wine which doesn't keep or travel very well. In his own country, in his own time, he was a superb salesman of himself. Beyond any question, he was enormously popular and much more loved than feared.

In this, of course, he would surely have caused the Florentine uneasiness. Machiavelli would have had an amused admiration for the impact of the act itself, and a certain fastidiousness at the absence of any hint of taste. But Machiavelli, despite his view that fear outruns gratitude every time, expressly approved the achievement of popularity, though he could never have imagined that a rabble of weavers or peasants could be made into a long-term, formidable weapon of politics. Such troops belonged with undesirables like Fra Girolamo Savonarola with his book-burnings and his unhealthy invocations of purity and religion. Mussolini is sometimes compared to another historic figure, Cola di Rienzo, the thirteenth-century phenomenon (Wagner's Rienzi) who for a brief season took and held Rome at the head of a crowd of low-caste supporters in the name of a resurrected Roman republic. Like Mussolini he had plebeian support, and like Mussolini he ended hung upside-down in a city square.

Aldo Parini, a friend from Mussolini's Socialist youth who never trimmed to join the victorious caravan where he would have been welcome, but who remained on affectionate terms with the Duce personally, said sadly to Mussolini's face that he feared that he would come to such a conclusion. 'This regime of yours, I am afraid, will end badly. Such things always do. Benito, you'll die like Cola di Rienzo.' It is not clear which takes the breath away more completely: the devastating accuracy of Parini's prediction or his ability to say such things to the supreme head of a Fascist state who responded only with a joke. Mussolini was, of course, a highly unsatisfactory Fascist. His rhetoric was full of blood and skulls and kicks in the stomach and there was a good deal of casual knocking-about in the early days; also, at the hands of Farinacci, the party general secretary and other under-ling bureaucrats, there was a good deal of prying and intrusion. But imagine any of the great men of the twenties and thirties responding as Mussolini did to a headline at once sycophantic and critical: 'Duce's excessive kindness to Zaniboni'. Zaniboni had tried to assassinate Mussolini many years earlier (in 1925). He had, instructively, not been executed. The really keen Fascists still hankered for a death. Mussolini's comment was 'Kindness can never be excessive.' That was near the end, up on Lake Garda with the world lost to him. But even in his pride of day, Mussolini was neither a murderer nor a totalitarian. He was a fake god and an actor–manager, with a god's conceit and an actor–manager's want of subtlety, but essentially he did not govern through fear. Rather, in the words which Samuel Johnson wrote as the prologue to a play by Garrick:

> The drama's laws the drama's patrons give
> And we that live to please must please to live.

Mussolini came unstuck, came into hatred and contempt, by going beyond the things he understood. To take credit for what government might very well have done under the least charis-matic, frock-coated, flat-voiced parliamentary functionary – a road opened, a malarial marsh drained, when roads had been opened and marshes drained before – was his especial talent. And with a managed press and radio, bombastic and inaccurate pieces

[180]

of economic and social optimism were under no fire. Just as Franco, a very different sort of man, taciturn, not keen on politics and truly, temperamentally, conservative as Mussolini never was, would survive the defeat of the Axis powers, so Mussolini might have done. He was, until very late, genuinely popular at home. And, unlike Franco, he had fought no war against his own country. The displays and the wide publicizing of slender reforms were excellent politics; but to go to war was to enter a market and see one's price fall.

In military matters the avoidance of hatred and contempt, concentration upon the show and display side of life, can lead to doing the actual job very badly. The tanks that Mussolini's armies took to North Africa were cheap tin objects which could be pierced by machine-gun fire. But since they were cheap, he could buy a lot of them, and being thinly armoured, they could be represented by the showman as highly manoeuvrable. For the march-past they looked fine and they served all purposes quite admirably – short of getting involved in anything rough like war. His planes, *per contra*, were of high quality but too few to be of military effect. His guns were built by the Austrians before the First World War; 'Biedermeier guns', Barzini calls them.

Italy was militarily equipped for talking about war. When, in the great folly of his lifetime, Mussolini actually engaged in it, he had the sham victories of Abyssinia, no glory in Albania and reversal in Greece.

For Mussolini to make war was like an operatic tenor being called upon to fight a real duel. The guns of the Communist partisans who shot him at the gates of the Villa Belmonte above Lake Garda were like those of the firing squad faced by Cavaradossi in *Tosca* – loaded! But when Mussolini's body swung upside-down in the Piazzale Loreto in Milan as Cola di Rienzo's had swung in Rome, it epitomized the frailty, the brittle quality of what he had been about. It was worse and more than he deserved, not that Machiavelli is troubled with deserts. At the end, Mussolini was an exhausted actor–manager who had started quoting from the wrong text, tragedy rather than pantomime, and deserved to be whistled off.

In his life's work of frantic activity, of proving his greatness to the masses in order to please them, he had become the hypnotized prisoner of his own purpose. Instead of coolly hoodwinking the crowd, he was under compulsion to perform, to attempt the unjumpable jumps. He was like George Orwell's famous description of the white man in Burma. Ostensibly he is the sahib and master with his gun, but he is obliged to shoot the elephant not because it is necessary but because the crowd expects it of him, of his sahib's status. Dictatorship, having given Mussolini position, obliged him to live up to it.

Mussolini was also brought by degrees into awful company. He had spoken slightingly of the novice Hitler, the drab man with an ill-fitting suit, so obviously awed and impressed by the Italian cabaret put on for his first visit. He was contemptuous and dismissive of the racial obsession in Hitler's speeches and writings. But Hitler did prove fascinating, not least in his devotion to Mussolini, sincere flattery being the most dangerous. No advice was ever given to the Duce more valuable than that of an exasperated old Italian diplomat. 'Which gases are most dangerous?' Mussolini asked him patronizingly after keeping him long in an ante-room. 'Incense,' said the ambassador, put on the retired list shortly afterwards.

The requirements of Machiavelli were finally not satisfied because Mussolini succeeded too well at pleasing and ended by delighting himself. As a journalist he was a booster, a writer of destiny-laden editorials, not a sneerer from the newsroom. For a journalist he lacked scepticism. Given wrong figures greatly overstating Italy's strength, he would query them, be told that no indeed, these were a mistake, be given others, also wrong but less nonsensical, and ask no more questions. Propagandists, like the retailers of white powders, are unwise to consume their own product.

No less unfortunate was the fact that Mussolini also persuaded

Hitler; and he put great trouble into the persuading. Six months' preparation preceded Hitler's visit in 1938; soldiers due to parade had been chosen for their 'Aryan' appearance. As with the provincial visits of British royalty, only more so, places were painted, indeed to the degree that streets came to look like film sets. Italy at this time had begun to resemble the Russia of Potemkin. As for the tin tanks, they did very well the one thing they were good for. And to take such anxious trouble for Hitler was to show judgement or lack of it.

Despite the pageantry, there were not lacking German generals who from prejudice or professional judgement would tell Hitler that Italy's military forces were lightweight, badly armed and to be discounted in any actual conflict. Hitler, so often right against professional and conventional judgement, was here resoundingly wrong. Convinced of the destiny and strength of the Axis – not, as he might quite realistically have been, of the ability of the German army to win a world war – he swept Mussolini along with him and would later lose vital time rescuing his ally from Balkan holes which professional and conventional wisdom would have foreseen. Mussolini should have stayed at home; Hitler should have left him there.

When the time came for Mussolini to fall, the short struggle in the Grand Council and the desertion of his son-in-law Count Ciano, Marshal Badoglio, the King and others demonstrated that the great game of presentation, the seeking to please and avoidance of contempt as a full-time vocation had come to an end. The deserters, like many deserters from causes, were rational men. They understood a lost war and meant to get out of it. They knew that they were on the wrong side, the losing one. Mussolini himself, back in 1939–40, hesitating, not wanting to jump, had thought in the same way as they now did. His old timidity was allied with a return of the lucidity which Hitler's triumphs and calls to war had wiped away. In the last melancholy part of his life, Mussolini, now a mere political expression, was once again placed to contemplate reality. But even debilitated and

defeated, his grasp upon such reality was restored. He understood the vanities which had destroyed him. In a strange
interview with the journalist Ivanoe Fossani he talked intensely,
but to the point: 'I heard the word "genius" a hundred times a
day.'

CHAPTER ELEVEN

How a prince must act to win honour: President George Bush and his followers in the Gulf War

(*The Prince* XXI)

'Nothing brings a prince greater prestige than great campaigns and demonstrations of his personal ability.' Machiavelli has a cool view that war, providing you win it, is good for you. He takes as his example Ferdinand of Aragon, a man whom he actively disliked for his sanctimoniousness, but admired for his grasp of what must be done. Ferdinand, said Machiavelli, had risen from a position of weakness to being 'the first king of Christendom'. In our time, Ferdinand would have stressed his devotion to the United Nations and related his acts to one of its resolutions (one of those which he accepted). In his own time, he made great play of being the Most Christian King of Spain and made war on Muslims for a catalogue of reasons. As King of Aragon he set about making himself King of Spain; as a Most Christian King and husband of the bigoted and shrilling Queen of Castile, he was attacking the enemies of Christ – almost, perhaps, for a quiet life. He was also, as Machiavelli spells out, making himself more secure at home. The barons of Castile, capable otherwise of making trouble for Ferdinand, were distracted and preoccupied. 'As they were giving their minds to the war, [they] had no mind for causing trouble at home. In this way, without their realizing what was happening, he increased his standing and his control over them.' Machiavelli takes a very north Italian view of Ferdinand's pious intentions. 'Under the same cloak of religion he assaulted Africa; he started his campaign in Italy; he has recently attacked France.' It was ever so. War is a handy diversion, religion or its working equivalent its most useful cover. Despite the exertions of American evangelists and a high level of aggressive sanctimony in that most powerful country, a war could not be undertaken by America, our most ready bringer of rockets and bombs, for purely theological reasons. What small, profitable wars most require today is a convenient identified enemy, a Spiderman squatting on 100 million screens, an evil to be preached against and comfortingly feared. It is a peculiar irony, after fifty years of twitchy and obsessive anti-communism, to find the picture of Emmanuel Goldstein:

As usual the face of Emmanuel Goldstein, the Enemy of the People, had flashed on to the screen. There were hisses here and there among the audience . . . The programmes of the two-minute hate varied from day to day, but there was none in which Goldstein was not the principal figure. He was the primal traitor, the earliest defiler of the Party's purity . . .

Winston's diaphragm was constricted. He could never see the face of Goldstein without a painful mixture of emotions. It was a lean Jewish face with a great fuzzy aureole of white hair and a small goatee beard – a clever face and yet somehow inherently despicable . . . And all the while lest one should be in any doubt as to the reality which Goldstein's specious claptrap covered, behind his head on the television there marched the endless columns of the Eurasian army – row after row of solid-looking men with expressionless Asiatic faces, who swam up to the surface of the screen and vanished, to be replaced by others exactly similar. The dull rhythmic tramping of soldiers' boots formed the background to Goldstein's bleating voice.

Before the hate had proceeded for thirty seconds, uncontrol-lable exclamations of rage were breaking out from half the people in the room . . . A hideous ecstasy of fear and vindictiveness, a desire to kill, to torture, to smash faces in with a sledge-hammer, seemed to flow through the whole group of people like an electric current turning one against one's will into a grimacing, screaming lunatic.

Allowing for the dramatic intensity of Orwell's account of a two-minute hate at a ministry gathering in Oceania in 1984, how different is the broad purpose of American television coverage or of the spaniel noises of the British *Times* and the flotilla of tabloid newspapers as they contemplate Saddam Hussein, as they have contemplated the late ruler of Iran, the Ayatollah Khomeini or, in a narrow British context, as we have considered the Argentinian generals or before them President Gamal Abdel Nasser?

To say this is not to doubt that the persons contemplated are unattractive, though a historic view of President Nasser will find a fundamentally decent man, ludicrously abused by those he disobliged. Incidentally, Orwell's description of Goldstein as a silly-clever sheep seems fair enough apropos the later Trotsky. But western governments do not exert comprehensive control over their publics. To make war and kill a lot of people, they need plausible justifications. These cannot be confected out of air and inclination. But once up and running, the campaign, as the advertisers call it, can induce perfect oblivion in the general public, can indeed numb all inhibition and conscience. At the very lowest estimate, 100,000 Iraqi soldiers were killed during the late American excursion; some put the numbers nearly twice as high. Few came from the élite Republican Guard of Emmanuel Goldstein/Saddam Hussein; most were conscripted soldiers without options. Quite enough of the casualties, like those shrivelled up in an air-raid shelter and described by Alfonso Rojo in the *Guardian* and *El Mundo*, were civilians caught up in the sort of 'whoops' occasions into which Americans at weapons controls seem just occasionally to slip.

No sense of unease, never mind wrong, was evident in crusading America or camp-following Britain. War was successfully made, glory gathered, a hundred bullfrogging headlines written, much allusion made to 'our boys'. The heroic idea was thought to have been put back into our drab little lives, and the reflected grandeur of our strong commanding ally was reflected upon with satisfaction. An American general, asked about casualties, expressed himself 'comfortable'. The degrading conduct of the American and British newspapers and broadcasts did not constitute a two-minute hate; it was neither so concentrated nor so absolute, dissent being tolerated. But the effects were identical, as was the corruption of mind: war gladly entered into (for the benefit of a sleazy but very rich associate, Kuwait, wired into a much richer and no less sleazy dependant and supplier, Saudi Arabia) and an all-round glow at force resoundingly employed, faces satisfyingly smashed, an enemy hit with hammers. And all this wins honour for the prince concerned.

The word 'honour' is not light. Machiavelli uses it in a very rational Italian way – as a commodity, something which will achieve authority with neighbours and deterrence against enemies. 'Let this prince use force and gain honour,' he says in effect, 'and he will be treated with a profitable circumspection.' But the word is worth pursuing down the lexical back lane. 'Honour', to the British after decolonization, loss of power and self-respect, went beyond Machiavelli's low and admirable grocer's view of it as so much pasta and salami. The British had been steadily humiliated, told to 'scram out of Africa'. They had devalued their currency, lost markets, seen black immigrants come and command citizenship. There existed a public-house consensus, in total agreement with the roadhouse consensus, that the lion had been teased, baited and humiliated enough and that his roar should be heard again. The invasion of Suez, undertaken by Anthony Eden, was intended to make that happen, though it took a Prime Minister temporarily enraged out of all judgement by an incompetent surgeon's errors. But the Prime Minister half-mad was echoed by a *Times* ever servile, the *Mail*, *Express*, *Telegraph*, his own party and most of the nation. Ferdinand of

Aragon would have seen the point of the war despite his extreme sanity.

Suez, however, failed for two reasons: a run on the currency and the United States's objection. British honour was nothing to the State Department which, for reasons of sentiment, had been willing to countenance British notions of greatness. Delusion would be dispelled, but the afterbreath of delusion lives on. In his chapter 21 Machiavelli gives advice to small powers about their relationships with great powers. It is very succinct advice: 'Agree with them at once, offer complete and unreserved compliance.' He cites the comment of the Roman legate during the invasion of Greece by Antiochus III. Antiochus had invited the Achaeans to stand aside as neutrals from the conflict. The Roman message to the Achaeans was that if they stood aside they would be without favour or dignity and would become the prize of the victor: *sine gratia, sine dignitate, praemium victoris eritis*. Britain's condition it is, largely through her earnest desire to attend top tables if only for coffee, to have become anyway the victor's prize and not one highly esteemed.

Britain and America herself could be excused some pique if not grief at events in the third quarter of the century. The old notion of western authority enforced by gunboats was much mocked by left-liberal commentators at home and by the rulers of former gunboat-receiving countries. The idea of intervention was out of fashion. For Britain it was past undertaking. For America the idea of such business did not die, though it became more covert, and a lexicon of euphemism was dreamt up to describe the actions of the United States government. The wiping-out of forests in order to kill more people, in the hope that some of them might be Viet Cong, was known as 'defoliation'. The acid showered over local populations was gaily titled 'Agent Orange'; an army of occupation and aggressively pursued war was 'the American advisers'. (By extension, shooting and burning constituted 'advice'.) In much the same spirit, American spies ('intelligence agents') who murder someone 'exercise extreme prejudice'.

In fairness, however, the wars waged and the acts of covert aggression and intervention in the affairs of other nations were not seen by American politicians as conferring useful honour, either in Machiavelli's sense or in the emotional sense favoured in Britain. The overthrow of a left-wing government in, say, Guatemala and its replacement by men who would have been at ease in the councils of the Sturmabteilung was hardly a question of the pursuit of honour. It was a combination of fear, arrogance and habit. That same combination would involve the United States in the internal affairs of most South and Central American countries, of South-east Asia and the entire Middle East. Amongst her allies were to be found Ferdinand Marcos, Ngo Dinh Diem and his thirteen successors, Augusto Pinochet ('an authoritarian not a totalitarian' in the immortal words of Jeane Kirkpatrick), the Shah of Iran and, let us never forget, Saddam Hussein.

Involvement in Vietnam demonstrated that honour is a complex thing, full of nuance. A war waged by unacknowledged troops against an unrecognized enemy, one waged without popular home support, by means which could not be looked in the eye, it fell short of doing the United States honour. The Machiavellian significance of the Vietnam War was the definition it spelt out of what wars may be waged, by what means and how long. It is a naïve liberalism which supposes that the response to the Vietnam War in a mighty turning-down of thumbs across America (and Europe, even Britain) owed much to morality. Morality, as ever, gave enormous pleasure and exercise to people who like that sort of thing. It didn't actually matter.

Popular revulsion against the Vietnam War was the result of failure, of not winning, of the war going interminably on and of large numbers of Americans dying. Begun as a serious conflict in the days of Kennedy and Camelot, causing the humiliation of his successor, Lyndon Johnson, the war was ended on the initiative of Richard Nixon, a vastly more intelligent statesman than prejudice allows, but not altogether the small voice of conscience. It was a war which Niccolò Machiavelli himself would not have hesitated to escape from. A shallow response to its conclusion was to suppose that it would make adventure unacceptable, but only the most naïve could have imagined that the invasion of other countries and the assumption of interim kingship around the globe might end. Rather, it was *long* involvements that became unacceptable, likewise the deaths of many Americans.

The outcome made the United States, even more than she was already, tactically minded. The phrase used recurringly by President Bush as his planes set out to bomb Baghdad was 'a surgical strike'. As much might be claimed by any wielder of an axe. But it was essential that the war should not linger on the public retina, that the goldfish attention-span of American indignation should not be put to stress and that the dead should be other people's. Such a war would be, necessarily, vicarious and highly technological. Killing over great distances is not less killing, but it feels different and is safer. Ethically, though of course we are not talking ethics, there is extreme difficulty in making a distinction between an explosive device sent by the very latest thing in rocketry some scores of miles to kill people and another left in a parcel at a railway station for the same purpose.

Eminent churchmen anxious to come up with the temporal goods have expounded on 'the just war' and on the defence of war generally. As a glaze added as part of the after-service to the killing such preachings do very well. But the purpose of explosives is to kill. And the purpose of FAE (ignited petrol vapour) is to burn before killing, thus instructing the witnesses of death altogether more soundly. A specific Christian reflection on the technique has not been sought.

The Gulf War showed all the lessons of Vietnam fully learnt. It was fought by way of overkill with the very best technology. The bombs fell first, armies engaged later; above all, it was quick. American rulers make war in the knowledge that their country lacks *Sitzfleisch*. Public acquiescence in a four-year slow catastrophe like the First World War is unimaginable to them after Vietnam. That may be a reflection of what we loosely call democracy, the vulnerability of men in uniforms and office to the displeasure of a voting citizenry, the lack of American faith in the all-wisdom of their leaders. If so, it is salutary, but it will only stop wars from going on, not from starting. And given modern means of delivery and destruction, an awful lot may be telescoped into a comparatively short time.

The purpose of this particular war would also have charmed Machiavelli. He knew from history, himself lived in and fully recognized, a world of major and minor powers. He saw the small powers much as he saw the mass of people: amoral onlookers professing anything and waiting to find out who was going to win. The rulers of Kuwait, whose sovereignty and integrity were the occasion of the war, might be an ignoble bunch of despots, inclined to torture. But they were very rich, reliable suppliers of oil and their successful protection told the rulers of Saudi Arabia, no nicer but very much richer and even bigger suppliers of oil, that the United States could be relied upon.

Few things, incidentally, were more instructive than the amazement of the politicians when, in the matter of the Kurds, they stumbled upon a cause actually appropriate to their liberationist rhetoric. And their early, blind inability to know what they should do or think was fascinating. Mr Major, in particular, let fall some unhappy and enlightening words of private irritation. He was not aware, he said, of having invited the Kurds to expose themselves to retribution. The Kurds, of course, had featured in the pre-war publicity build-up. They had appeared in all the hand-outs and on the PR video. They had, monstrously, been gassed in large numbers by Hussein. When they *were* gassed six years earlier, no denunciation was entered or public protest made at the United Nations by those who were now the crusaders against Saddam Hussein. For at that moment the crusaders had been the tyrant's well-wishers, armers and associates. The fact that the Kurds were also being ill-treated and discriminated against (more modestly) by Turkey and Syria – Muslim participants in this crusade – was an excellent reason for keeping concern for them as a purely ornamental affair, a flourish of grace-notes on the main theme.

Unsympathetic people might also point out that in one phase of the Kurds' long history of persecution they were being bombed by the British for rather unpious reasons of uncomplicated power-seeking in 1919. By 1991, the British, caught by their own public opinion, were driven to make a short-breathed exertion for the Kurds with the 'enclave' notion. But the Kurdish tragedy illuminates the gap between real reasons for fighting a small war – oil, money, client-assurance, bravado and figure-cutting – and those put on display: civilization, hostages, the rule of law, peace (after war) and 'our moral duty'.

One sometimes wonders, fleetingly, why politicians do not say these things outright. For George Bush to have argued coolly and truthfully the reasons why a small war with a manageable number of dead made excellent policy would have saved him a mighty volume of pious exhalation. Such clarity is alien to politicians, at least partly because to speak plain at large involves speaking plain to themselves. To do that is to acknowledge and proclaim what it is second nature not to acknowledge. Even Stalin understood discretion. Who would kill when he could 'eliminate'? And in the great Soviet culls, it was never men who were eliminated, only 'elements'.

Euphemism and atrocity are irresistibly attracted to each other. The tone of Machiavelli's account of Ferdinand, the asperity of a candid man towards a humbug, doesn't alter the fact of Ferdinand's modernity. No public relations adviser could have bettered the Aragonese king's promotion of an ostensibly confessional war undertaken in fact for the purposes of (a) self-aggrandizement and (b) the confusion and distraction of his internal opponents. The high tone is essential; even Hitler found it necessary to stage a fake incident at a Polish border-post before his September invasion.

But for 'God and the Church' now read 'the United Nations'. This is an institution with which Machiavelli never had to cope, though it would have given him hours of pleasure. It exists in principle for the achievement of 'world government', something in which nobody believes except cranks, legalistic pedants and people who think they are going to be doing the governing. The UN was kept usefully absurd during the forty years of two-power control, the Soviet Union and the USA poised like heraldic beasts on either side of a bricked-up door. United Nations general secretaries (apart from the ambitious, high-minded Swede, Dag Hammarskjöld who embodied a little of all three above-listed characteristics of a believer, made trouble and died suddenly), spent terms of office collecting their salaries, wringing their hands, being photographed getting out of aeroplanes and issuing appeals for peace like so many popes. They were the curators of an abstract aspiration.

With the collapse of the Soviet Union in the dignified, grave and incapable hands of Mr Gorbachev, the circumstances of the UN changed out of recognition. Military strength is what matters, with wealth and production at its elbow. Japan matters, Germany matters, Saudi Arabia matters, the United States matters. But Japan has had an aloof tradition of cultivating its garden since it last played on a Try-Your-Strength machine, and has sold its flowers and vegetables to the world in the most satisfactory manner. Germany is wary and still shock-tinged after forty years, inclines to Scandinavian virtue painted by numbers, and anyway makes a mess of its few foreign excursions (witness the recognition of Croatia and Bosnia, a cause of war which could have been explained to them). As for Saudi Arabia, she is a backward state firmly anchored in the eighth century and smart enough to know it. The policy of not moving at all in order not to fall apart is wisely followed.

The rest of the world, apart from specific local delinquents, is made up of followers; and they follow. Consequently, if the United States were to press the Security Council and Assembly for a declaration of war on Jupiter, this would, after minor recalcitrances, be forthcoming. The United States is the United Nations because no one else wants to be.

Accordingly America's decisions to drop bombs, fire rockets, kill people and impose her will across boundaries have as fine and high a moral varnish to them as fifteenth-century Catholic Christianity could confer upon the seizure of Granada or the later driving-out of Jews. Listen to a droning speech by an American cabinet officer or his British body-servant and you will hear the resolutions of the United Nations intoned like a liturgy. What we have here is law plus religion, everything done by due forms, all the papers countersigned and tied up. It would be a mistake to think that this does not matter to the participants, especially the chief movers. Legal form, like the word of God, confers a quiet mind and a title to what is taken. How else could one kill so many human beings and ignite an oilfield in order to recover a small tract of good geology from one despot on behalf of another?

The talk is of 'alliance', meaning in practice unconvinced Germans, Italians hoping to get something, and the British proving something to themselves. The notion of Alliance is sought by the warmaker as spreading the moral equity and making a private, self-interested act seem both public and disinterested. Thus the USA drew Australia and South Korea into the Vietnam War and made serious efforts to pull in Great Britain who, astonishingly, did not go. The difference between now and then is of course the difference between success and failure. Vietnam was exactly the sort of war one does not join, except for immediate self-interest which both South Korea and Australia had or thought they had – the prevention of communist hordes from marching over fallen dominoes to seize the rest of South Asia and Australia. Japan, a more circumspect and wiser cookie, thought no such thing.

On the other hand, the evidence of the Gulf War and of the British expedition to the Falklands is that small wars are excellent business. Assuming military competence – not an easy matter for the Americans who delicately balance superlative technology with personal ineptitude and ready flashes of cowardice – the seeker of honour impresses across eight weeks of talk and maybe ten days of killing that in fights he wins. This is something which has weighed with man since the Stone Age, which an American general contemplated bombing enemies back to. He shows important clients that he can deliver and his own voters that theirs is a truly great country ('a lionhearted people' – Mrs Thatcher).

In Britain the Falklands was wonderful business. We had suffered more than humiliations. As a nation, we had been in long, sustained secular decline. Our needs were consequently deeper than those of the USA, though that country indulges a louder, more tasteless and depressing patriotism than Britain, whose apathetic nature mutes the impulse to folly. But given the chance to make war, we seized it. We exulted in the (genuine) skill and courage of soldiers and sailors, felt the charm of war – of hanging upon bulletins, of getting awful feelings in the pit of the stomach, even of losing engagements. The *Sir Galahad* and *Sheffield* incidents – by reason of odd twists in the British psyche, which likes a good cry, or in this case a good retch because faces were burned off – were almost more important than Tumbledown.

Americans, rich in their inheritance of resources, easily paced in respect of their enemies from the Iroquois onwards, a spoiled people with a taste for tantrums and a cult of self, expect victory and scream when denied it. The British, although contemptuous of foreigners as comic or unreal, have historically been served victory late after a long menu of defeat. It has made them masochists, and the Falklands War yielded plenty for masochists to enjoy. But we did win, and what we took from the war was honour rather in the old sense of the word: pride in ourselves – a sense of having done right and then come through after a morally necessary spot of suffering. In Machiavelli's and Ferdinand's sense, we didn't need such honour and had no practical use for it. It was too late to give us standing and route us towards tangible power. Neither it nor anything would mend our bust economy; bankers would do the same sums and add in the hard costs of war. But of course politically honour was a pretty penny for the Thatcher government to turn.

And to the British more generally, it mattered as private assurance that what they had been, they still might be. That this war was fought for two mist-hung mudflats in the South Atlantic inhabited by slow-spoken Scottish sheep-farmers, that it supported those sheep on its grade 5 land at a ratio of 13 acres to the animal, did not matter. That the government had tried to give the islands up, had planted in *The Times* an article entitled 'These Paltry Islands', that the heroic government of Mrs Thatcher was directly and in every particular to blame for the initial invasion through its diplomatic mix of hints to the Argentinians and undisguised contempt for the Falklanders, that the whole operation very well measured the expedition of Fortinbras for a territory – a straw which would not pay the burial of its dead – was all very well and we knew it at heart. But the war still made the British feel good, made their incompetent government look good for re-election, and made their class-war-fighting, three-million-unemployed-inducing ranter of a lady prime minister look even better, since a state of war so perfectly chimed in with her emotional condition. It *didn't* matter; it wasn't, as the Gulf War was for the USA, practically useful; but it brought enormous solace.

In the case of Mr Bush, thanks to deplorable timing, the Gulf War did not deliver the election victory universally predicted, then and after, as its consequence. But that mistake will hardly be repeated; and few people have played the rest of their cards quite as badly as Mr Bush. His final indulgence in a late encore merely shows him up as having been the prisoner of his own high-mindedness. The making of war had made him popular and respected within America and its circle as nothing before or since, and he seemed with the threats and flyovers of January 1993 to be reminding himself how it felt. Mr Clinton's war will be better arranged.

CHAPTER TWELVE

A prince's personal staff and *How flatterers must be shunned*: The contrasted experience of Harold Wilson and Margaret Thatcher

(*The Prince* XXII and XXIII)

We are rather spoiled by the Italian sixteenth century. No political tableau is complete without poisoned wine, stiletto-play or a garrotting. English domestic politics, even under Mrs Thatcher, cannot yield such colourful excess. Execution as a political sanction went out with Lord Lovat in 1746. The worst low to which a statesman can fall in our system is a seat on the back-benches or perhaps the Department of Energy.

Nevertheless, the soft-handed and quotidian nature of constitutional and democratic politics does not invalidate Machiavelli's judgements. A prime minister, even one forbidden to strangle opponents, is today a prince, sometimes (witness Margaret Thatcher) one as imperious and peremptory as any affectation of escutcheons or descent from Charlemagne could have made her. And underlings are still underlings. What Machiavelli refers to as 'ministers' today embraces advisers, cronies and indeed whole governments, i.e. cabinet ministers. And to them applies most of what concerned Machiavelli in chapters 22 and 23 of *The Prince*, which deal in apt order with ministers and flatterers.

The choosing of ministers is of no little importance to a prince;

and their worth depends on the sagacity of the prince himself. The first opinion that is formed of a ruler's intelligence is based on the quality of the men he has around him. When they are competent and loyal he can always be considered wise, because he has been able to recognize their competence and keep them loyal. But when they are otherwise the prince is always open to adverse criticism; because his first mistake has been in the choice of his ministers.

Machiavelli makes his case with the example of Messer Antonio da Venafro, minister to Pandolfo Petrucci, the Prince of Siena. 'No one who knew Venafro could help but conclude that this prince was a man of great ability.' A man may understand a thing for himself, may understand what others can understand or he can comprehend neither. The second sort of intelligence is good enough. To hire a Venafro who would get things right for you was intelligence enough in a ruler.

On the other hand, a prince must be on his guard against the ambitions of ministers when they start putting their interests ahead of his. Machiavelli then makes a judgement highly congenial to certain recent national leaders: 'a man entrusted with government must never think of himself, but of the prince and must never concern himself with anything but the prince's affairs.' His natural self-interest, in the affable Florentine view, is best seen off by feeding. The prince must 'pay him, honour, enrich him, put him in his debt, share with him both honours and responsibilities'.

In modern government most of these precautions are built into the system. Enrichment is not advised, however, being confined at present to the children of the prince, who may, through adept promenading of them by interested parties as mascots in the circles of arms dealers and Middle Eastern rulers, acquire a pleasant competence. An exception to the general ministerial austerity has been the ability of ministers to assume high positions (gloriously salaried) in public utilities which they had legislated into private ownership. But for the most part, we handle the standing of ministers in the manner of a court. Official ministers receive the equivalent of sixteenth-century court honour and precedence through the in-house deference of the British Civil Service (which is drilled to say 'Minister' or 'Secretary of State', not 'Mr Smiggs'). Norman Tebbit's driver expressed herself uninterested in the precise identity of his first full department, Employment. 'What matters is that we got the Daimler.'

Grace and glory are great things in politics and in Britain; they are distributed with a delicate sense of increment, the Secretary of State travelling by a better marque of limousine, looking at rather more borrowed pictures, drinking tea from a finer china than a minister of state. Grandeur comes on draught and graded. For outside advisers, very reluctantly admitted into the bloodstream of office at first, forms of distinction are less clear. But their relationship is a personal one. They live by the prince's love or necessity.

What Machiavelli says about ministers obtains today, as do his judgements in the following chapter on the avoidance of flatterers. Advisers, cronies, ministers and flatterers tend to blur and merge, flattery being often an important aspect of advice. For the followers of Mrs Thatcher who at regular intervals burst into tears – at her reproaches or her fall – there was a further blurring between flattery and abject devotion beyond the demands of a Renaissance court. The impression was given by some younger admirers and attendants that had the lady demanded their impalement upon the highest sharp pinnacle of the Westminster clock-tower, they would unfailingly have given what President Lincoln called 'this last full measure of devotion' and that she would have been sincerely touched.

But flattery is an aspect of all government; it is readily given and delightedly consumed. The best advice remains that of Adlai Stevenson, truest wit and stylist of American politics: 'Flattery is all right', he said, 'as long as you don't inhale.' Machiavelli observed that 'the only way to safeguard yourself against flatterers is by letting people understand that you are not offended by the truth'. This, however, is altogether too much of a good thing: 'if everyone can speak the truth to you then you lose respect.' That phrase deserves to be rolled around the mouth and savoured, since it perfectly defines the position of any holder of power. Truth diminishes respect. Sensibly, Machiavelli called for a compromise between flattery and truth by confining candid speech to an élite of chosen advisers and, even with them, authorizing it only in matters where the prince seeks their advice. A sort of moral monetarism requires truth to keep its value by means of limited circulation.

He also said something else, well enough illustrated in our own time. 'A prince must always seek advice but he must do so when he wants to not when others want him to . . . All the same he should be a constant questioner and should listen patiently to the truth regarding what he has enquired about . . . Here is an infallible rule: a prince who is not himself wise cannot be well advised.' He can, of course, take on a single very able adviser, says Machiavelli, and this fellow will get things right for him – but that man will end by trying to take over from him. 'Things cannot be otherwise since men will always do badly by you unless they are compelled to be virtuous. So the conclusion is that good advice, whomever it comes from, depends on the shrewdness of the prince who seeks it, and not the shrewdness of the prince on the good advice.'

Few princes could have more different experiences of their court than Harold Wilson and Margaret Thatcher. Wilson took as his official political cabinet an outstanding group of talents. People of the quality of Denis Healey, Anthony Crosland and Roy Jenkins seemed then to grow on trees. He had no dominant intellectual mentor, no voice outside the Civil Service or official politics outlining a political or economic direction.

His kitchen cabinet, on the other hand, contained two economists, Nicholas Kaldor and Thomas Balogh, the latter a notably silly man, both much pilloried in the mildly ill-natured way of England for foreignness. However, the burden of these two men's advice was too radical for the Prime Minister's conventionality. His personal secretary, Marcia Williams, his press officers, Gerald Kaufman and later Joe Haines, were important – Williams enormously so. But they were important to the Prime Minister's life rather than to the substantial conduct of policy. The political cabinet quarrelled; indeed it quarrelled (and intrigued) as much as any parcel of ministers this century.

The people dominating the Prime Minister's time, his principal ministers, were mindful always of their personal advantage and of the possibility of one of them ultimately taking Wilson's position and the others advancing theirs. They were not, as in the case Machiavelli speaks of, contributing so much that they might come to threaten him. Wilson was not burdened by their usefulness, but they threatened him just the same. George Brown, for one, was a man of disputed ability, but important as the leader of a faction, the Labour right. He was charming and interesting but also emotionally unstable, liable to produce resignation threats as a cow gives milk, paranoid and alcohol-enveloped. Ironically, about one central thing, the most important issue of all, he was right.

Brown, at the short-lived Department of Economic Affairs, early favoured a devaluation or, better, a flotation of the currency. The pound was under recurring and destructive pressure from speculation; and great energies and resources were expended in a three-year struggle (1964–7) to sustain it. The Treasury believed that devaluation was a bad thing, injurious by way of inflation and anyway an easy way out. They advised the difficult way out.

In this they were served by James Callaghan, Chancellor of the Exchequer. Callaghan was a splendidly impressive, narrowly effective politician, astute, avuncular, ruthless. He was invariably calm and always sober. Unlike Brown he inspired confidence and notions of solid, competent reliability; and unlike

Brown he was wrong. In Machiavelli's terms he was no threatening man of brilliance, rather of comforting mediocrity who adheres. Succeed he did, but no one would have killed Harold to make Jim king. Tied hand and foot to the Treasury who understood and got wrong what he did not understand, he resisted devaluation/flotation across three years of ever-fiercer bouts of speculation. He made cuts in areas dear to his party and expended reserves to a degree modest only by comparison with the more celebrated expenditures of Mr Lamont, for the purpose of stopping what eventually, in a state of abject despair, he would concede. Upon a policy of floating the pound, steady and strong growth might well have been sustained; as might the reputation of a government which thirty months after devaluation would lose in an election its majority of 100.

After a brief period of eclipse and bruised reputation, Callaghan would re-emerge – he was a notably conservative and unremarkable Home Secretary – as the man who by reason of stability, reliability, strength of character and soundness, was Wilson's obvious and only possible successor. During his period of consolidation (as Home Secretary, 1967–70), he led the opposition to the government's trade-union policy, known as 'In Place of Strife', which proposed moderate reductions in trade-union immunities. If it had passed into law, this moderate reform might easily have prevented the extreme anti-trade-union policies of Mrs Thatcher. Lacking the provocation of union excesses, her ferocious notions would not have come on to the agenda. A Labour government passing such reforms would have won credit for courage, would have pre-empted aggressive anti-unionism and faced up to a problem.

With assured common-sense dogmatism, James Callaghan opposed reform in its entirety, arguing for an indefensible status quo as the only thinkable state of affairs, winning extensive trade-union support and backing within the parliamentary party, and humiliating and depressing the Prime Minister. In the process, the idea of his stability, reliability, strength of character and soundness became irresistible, and the foundations of his succession as perhaps the last Labour Prime Minister assured. One might add that in assessing the public sort of ministers, competence is never necessarily a major consideration. Callaghan was monstrously wrong (and notably reactionary over such things as immigration); but he possessed qualities of reassurance, normality and four-squareness. They were expressed in a sort of naval bluffness, in which 'steady as she goes' described a condition of being all at sea. Callaghan could travel on more than water. Like many an itinerant swami, he had the art of levitation.

Ministers in Wilson's government did indeed conspire and jockey. Brown, Callaghan and Jenkins were all seen by themselves and their supporters as potential replacements for the Prime Minister. The episode of the trip of Moscow, when Wilson came back shortly after the humiliation of actual devaluation to find that active conversations about his future had taken place, is a good instance. The Wilson government was a warren, not just of aspirers but of factions: former followers of Wilson's predecessor Hugh Gaitskell, the left of the party, and the private grouping which Callaghan drew around him from the middle and void of the party. (He was at all times the preferred option of its dullest members, the incarnation of its inadequacies.)

The Wilson figure who most caught attention, however, was Marcia Williams. There is precedent for a secretary or a woman influencing a statesman. Frances Stevenson, secretary, mistress and ultimately, by way of dying tribute, wife and countess to Lloyd George, was an intelligent and indispensable prop and adviser – and being a sensible, intelligent lady, very useful. Machiavelli, enthusiastic about violence, is reticent about sex. Mistresses do not much figure in *The Prince*. But he would have been yet more fastidious about the emotional dependence which, rather than physical attachment, linked Wilson with Mrs Williams.

Ben Pimlott, one of Wilson's two biographers, describes the

way in which Williams came to dominate the Prime Minister: shouting and screaming at him in front of witnesses – the equivalent he says, of hand-slapping – saying, 'You stupid boy' and offering both reproof when he was too pleased with himself and criticism when he didn't perform to satisfaction. This is not the place, if indeed any place is, for Freudian witter about fixations. As for Renaissance Florence, it acknowledged no alienism and did not indulge its great men with analysis, thinking in flat terms of winning and losing, power and the lack of it. But it recognized weakness and there was enough of that here. Reasonably obviously, Wilson was a weak, bulliable man; he may actually have enjoyed being bullied, so that his intelligence was vitiated by an impulse to submit. As evidently, Williams was, not to be nice about such things, a harridan and a scold. Much might be said for having her ducked in a pond, or better, drowned. It was not that she was not devoted or very hard-working, she was both. It was not that her political interventions were harmful or important. According to biographical opinion, she was middling-to-left in her views, not especially sophisticated or at all expert, but something of a left-wing recusant, keeping faith with old beliefs at a time when principles of any sort were lightly worn.

She did, however, exercise influence in terms of personalities and channels of authority. She had a bitter quarrel with the Prime Minister's private secretary, a young, fast-track civil servant working directly to Wilson. This was Derek Mitchell, a widely liked and valued man doing his job and, as Pimlott puts it, 'a discreet but ardent Labour supporter'. The subject of the quarrel was pitiful: Williams took exception to the typists, the 'Garden Room girls'. They were deemed by her to be middle-class, Conservative-inclined enemies – a touch here of Mrs Thatcher's 'not one of us' approach. Mitchell wrote a sharp note to Wilson in defence of their professionalism. There followed a bitter exchange between Mitchell and Williams. He later gave his estimate of her views:

It was obvious where the leanings of the No. 10 staff were and this was something which would have to be dealt with . . . it was in line also with the fact that the Civil Service as a whole was doing all it could to obstruct the Labour government . . . and that . . . the only solution would be to 'purge' No. 10 and so make sure that only people sympathetic to the government worked there; nothing else would do.

This was an insane way to think and an extension into real politics of all the paranoia and self-preoccupation of office politics. Such an aspiration of the clerical to lord it over the executive suggests an executive vulnerable and tyrannizable by any exertion of will. And in this conflict Mitchell was the loser: his term of service in Downing Street went no further than 1966, two years in all; and the most senior civil servant, Sir Laurence Helsby, who had fiercely opposed any blurring of the outsider/civil service demarcation, also made an early departure.

Machiavelli may not have had an office dragon in mind when he spoke of princes being judged on the strength of their advisers. But people − civil servants, cabinet ministers and journalists, friendly and hostile − did just that; they saw Williams and judged Wilson. They made a final judgement in the matter of 'the lavender list'. At the end of his time as Prime Minister, Wilson, like all retiring heads of government, issued resignation honours. They went to an unattractive group for the most part; though the ennoblement of ready money by spray-can at the hands of Mrs Thatcher puts Wilson's selection into long, very nigh invisible perspective. However, this group of rich cronies − one of whom would commit suicide on the eve of scandalous bankruptcy and yet another of whom was honest, foolish Marcia Williams herself − first appeared on a sheet of the secretary's lavender-coloured notepaper (something reported by Wilson's press secretary Joe Haines, whose own second (ill-) nature also reflected upon the man who hired him). The authorship of the honours list (it was written in Williams's hand and amended in Wilson's), led to undignified public outbursts by both and to open season in the Conservative press. It became a national topic and worse, a by-word. The lavender list became a phrase to sum up the anti-Wilson view of the government as shabby, corrupt and off-colour. Looked at dispassionately, it was none of these things. Rather was Wilson a kindly, put-upon and socially insecure man, easily taken advantage of by a circle of rather brazen third-division businessmen who flattered him and made him feel comfortable. Lord Kagan, Sir Eric Miller and the distinctly grander (distinctly Tory, respectable and Premier division) Sir James Goldsmith who made Williams a director of one of his companies, were seen as benefactors but certainly not of Wilson. Wilson was made to look, yet again, naïve, weak and bossed-about, not impressions which, as events conclude and the record-gathering commences, any statesman should end with. The lavender list marked such an end. It was neither bang nor whimper, but a sharp, amazed exhalation of breath.

The trouble with Williams, and it was a disastrous trouble, was that she destroyed credit. It was widely put about that she must be Wilson's mistress. Now for what it is worth, she almost certainly was not. But to put it Frenchly, a straightforward functioning sexual partner would have been no more objection-able than a steady supply of chocolate. The injurious aspect of mistresses is not the sex but the emotional ties, the upsets, the emotional disorientation, the general condition of distraction. With Lloyd George, who seems to have been able to have sexual intercourse without taking the pipe out of his mouth, none of these things applied. Equally, if Wilson had kept, as he certainly did not, a woman labelled, army-style, 'sexual intercourse for the purpose of', life would have been much easier for everyone.

There are only two objections to sex in a politician: envy and ridicule. Envy, the dislike of somebody doing something we fancy doing ourselves, is not a profound objection; but ridicule, the element of absurdity which emerges in the form of endear-ments, quirks, minor fetishes and that general condition of being naked and unarmed – the prophet in bed, as it were – which, once revealed in a gossipy press, does enormous harm, can in fact destroy a political figure entirely. When, in earlier times, there was a deadly penalty to pay for the fact of a liaison (never mind a felony like buggery), because society abominated the act, society was not told. When there is an easier climate, society is more readily tolerant of the act, told more and liable instead to split its sides over the small change, the Squidgy bits, Mrs Parker-Bowles's trousers, Chelsea FC shirts *und so weiter*. If Wilson had been attended by either a bright, discreet woman like Frances Stevenson or a functioning cutie who kept her mouth shut, who could have complained?

From Marcia Williams, government and prime-ministerial self-respect got the worst of all possible worlds: a shrill, hectoring, public-row-creating screamer – everything that marriage or concupiscence may sometimes carry with them as a price to be paid, but delivered without the advantages of either, a sort of non-playing captain. There was talk about sex without the consolations of sex; and worse, much worse, there was emotional involvement (not something to which any statesman hoping to be taken seriously should ever surrender).

We have foolishly, but for sure, a notion of politicians that since they lead us, they suffer no leading themselves. The idea is of strong, noisy men who admit to no needs, no tears, no cravings, no dependence on sympathy and love. The idea is a perfect nonsense, of course: its requirements are either unfulfillable or met only by half-psychopaths deficient in human responses. It has been actually a contributing cause to the cult of the strong man, the man on the white horse, the superhuman godling who will lead us from our shadows. It isn't an accident that Adolf Hitler made much of his indifference to women, or that all the dictators had their metallic qualities stressed. Man of Steel or Iron Lady, it's all sham metallurgy, a stupid hero-worship in which the hero is first worshipper. Nor was it an accident that General Georges-Ernest Boulanger, a prototype of the species and near-putschist in France a century ago – actually a man on a *black* horse – shot himself (at the grave of his mistress) in consequence of the misery of trying to achieve such barbarous and basalt status, having recognized himself as a human being.

But since we do think such nonsense, if only in the domesticated, pussy-cat, constitutional sense which wants charisma rather than argument, it doesn't help if a politician is rudely and noisily exposed as weak, loving, dependent, enslaved and mildly potty in a relationship. It is a failure of the heroic, a trembling of the stiff lip, an intimation of mortality which the public show cannot permit. The entire Williams connection caused the Prime Minister, a man of great gifts, application and decent purpose, to be laughed at; than which in government there is no greater tragedy, since it ends in the victim's despairing of himself.

A prince may get anything wrong, be any kind of transgressor, but he holds on to dignity, to respect, to caste, like an overboard mariner to a spar. We don't use the word 'prince' lightly. Machiavelli spoke it literally, but all holders of power have about them a piece of the mantle of princeliness. They are dignified as well as useful, they are ornamental, they are emblematic, they are part of magic. And to laugh at them is to withdraw belief in the magic, to treat the eucharist as cheap claret. Laugh at them and they slowly fade. Like Bunbury they are exploded and like Bunbury they have to die.

Wilson's government could have survived the failure to devalue early, could have survived the wretched faction-fighting and the clamorous ambitions which made the cabinet into one of life's less well-conducted rat-pits, could have survived James Callaghan. But it could not survive the seeping of respect from its prince, the decay of his standing under derision, of giggling death. Which is why the very least that well-wishers of Mr Wilson's government should have done was to knock Mrs Williams on the head on a dark night.

The comparison with Mrs Thatcher and *her* chief crony, Sir Alan Walters, shows, on the surface, great difference from

Williams's case. We are describing a professor of economics, an expert holding views, who in varying degrees got them across and influenced policy. There was not the same pathetic quality of emotional dependence, though in hard times Mrs Thatcher found herself lost without the prop of the professor, who was to become a telephonically linked ally. Professor Walters, when interviewed for TV, was commonly depicted on a sun-terrace in California where he had moved to better-remunerated cerebration. His place beneath the oleanders at the Pacific edge came to represent the furthest rim to which any entourage based in London has ever been pushed. He is, by his sharply flashing lights, a good economist and his views were close to hers. But other monetarists exist, alas, and it is odd to require the constant support of a single Professor twelve thousand miles away – though as a place for having a sustained friendly relationship with Mrs Thatcher it sounds like roughly the right distance.

In fact, Walters as a presence must be judged under two headings: as a technician giving influential advice whose rightness or wrongness is what matters, and as a personality upon whom the Prime Minister was seen to rely and whose interplay with her became a constitutional issue to the press and to cabinet ministers in the latter part of her era. Walters's first claim upon history and national admiration is that he, more than any other person, adviser, cabinet member or civil servant, brought about the massive monetary deflation of 1981. Then Whitehall-based, he argued in advance of the budget that only a huge take-out of public money would defeat inflation. He specified £5 billion. The Chancellor, Geoffrey Howe, started at one billion and was unwilling to go beyond one and a half.

For a long period in the key discussions Mrs Thatcher accepted the Chancellor's view, which was that of the Treasury as a whole. The debate took the form of Thatcher telling Walters that he didn't understand politics and that there were limits to how much of his theory was politically acceptable. Walters responded in his rough-genial East Midlands way by saying, 'I may know nothing about politics, Prime Minister, but I can do my sums, and if you don't go the distance no smaller reduction in circulating money will have any effect.' He was largely alone in this argument though he was to be joined by Peter Middleton, at this time a Treasury civil servant of low seniority (though Mrs Thatcher would later change that).

Walters's main ally, however, was Keith Joseph, often and wrongly derided, but the most attractive of the Tory right and powerfully influential with the Prime Minister. He, in Walters's account, was asked to approach her and seek to turn the key in the lock. He agreed, and the report is of a transformed Margaret Thatcher springing on cabinet and Geoffrey Howe the injunction: 'I want five billions out of the budget and I don't care if you have to raise standard rate [income tax].' Even though the final cut was more like three and a half billions, clearly the man who can get this done, even at second hand, is influential. Whether it *ought* to have been done is another matter. In the view of many, the application of that sort of apache monetarism was the direct cause of the first great Thatcher deflation and of three million unemployed – something which, when coupled with an average growth rate for the regime of 1.8 per cent, looks expensive.

Ian Gilmour, in his fine polemic and memoir *Dancing with Dogma*, points out that it was another monetarist economist, the Swiss professor Jürg Niehans, who observed that in any measure of the money supply, real life – falling sales, disappearing jobs, increased bankruptcies – demonstrated the level of money in circulation, and if the M3 figures said something else, the M3 figures were wrong. As Gilmour puts it: 'They had, in other words, made a terrible mistake, and in consequence had caused, quite unnecessarily, far and away the worst recession since the war.' He also quotes Keynes to the effect that deflation does not reduce wages automatically. 'It reduces them by causing unemployment. The proper object of dear money is to check an incipient boom. Woe to those whose faith leads them to aggravate a depression.'

In fairness to Walters, he had been quicker than Mrs Thatcher to see that the goose had been overcooked. His massive fiscal cuts came at this moment and substituted the public-sector borrowing requirement for M3. It was astute politics, it buried monetarist measures, it looked tough to please the blood culture of the City of London and for that reason permitted a further reduction of interest rates already down 2 per cent. Whether it should also be considered good economics is less clear. David Howell, a minister at this time, spoke of 'a sort of Stalingrad, the moment when the dark forces of public expenditure were finally and heroically turned'. In the view of Gilmour there was a 'growth recession' – an average annual growth of 2.8 per cent between 1981 and 1985 while unemployment grew by a third (three-quarters of a million) to a high point in mid-1986. That growth has to be contrasted with the 2.4 per cent of the Labour years, achieved with unemployment only briefly seen as high as one million. And Gilmour added that what was achieved came entirely from the ending of inventory run-downs. Stockbuilding had been *minus* six billion (annualized) in the last quarter of 1980, something which had to be reversed. There was also the matter of going from credit to dearth to the subsequent credit boom, which was itself to have calamitous long-term consequences.

On balance, in his capacity as adviser Walters emerges as shrewder politically than economically. He knew when something he approved of was not working and he pointed to a way out of it which disguised the harm it did through capital cuts and disemployment by using a credit boom and restocking to bring a tubercular bloom to the face of the economy. This was not a policy which could be called good or wise, but one which could pass on paper for successful – until it failed.

Now there are thus good Machiavellian reasons for approving Professor Walters. Good government is not part of the brief; successful government, which here means deftly evading the deserved consequences of bad government, is our preoccupation. If, after all, one can precipitate unemployment of three million-plus twice in one administration and link both occurrences with a consumer boom of the least advisable sort and yet talk miracles and win elections, then surely high-gloss semblance has beaten reality to the punch and created greatness in a prince. In the short term, this is true; but to amend Keynes, in the long run we are all found out. And Walters's cleverness looks likely to join most of the Thatcher government's reputation in inexorable decline. Its highest credit will be for pioneer work in establishing a new threshold for the acceptability of unemployment, and for the consequent two-track record of a government able to fail as a government and succeed as a political party at the same time.

Nevertheless, if Walters was politically effective, in many respects he was also a source of conflict and in ways not very different from those of Marcia Williams. All politics has a schoolroom quality, with access to teacher's love and attention at its heart. Marcia Williams was roundly told by the Chief Whip, Robert Mellish, that she was *no sodding good* when she barred his way to Harold Wilson. Nigel Lawson, Thatcher's second Chancellor, must have felt as much in his heart when, in the late eighties, he found himself second-guessed, privately consulted against, and at the last openly derided on television when, fronting the Californian oleanders, the professor known to be advising the Prime Minister mocked the delusions of her Chancellor.

Again, as to the rightness of the views occasioning the dispute, one may argue. Lawson believed in using exchange rates to guide the pound. His actual effort, the shadowing of the Deutschemark, was not happy. The mark was too strong and British notions of the country's economic miracle and the currency it had created were blithely unreal. The reasons for Britain's return to full recession after the Lawson boom years run far deeper than the one year of shadowing the Deutschemark. But Walters's public opposition to this single policy, even if right, did his mistress unimaginable political harm. Equally, his opposition to the Exchange-Rate Mechanism (ERM), which looks right when we have been in and had to come out, is dubious in that he opposed entry when the parity was much lower and membership sustainable. Arguably, the policy in which he encouraged the Prime Minister from his place in the sun had a result doubly disastrous – once for us, once for her. By resisting membership at a sensible low parity, the two of them split the inner cabinet of senior ministers more grievously than at any time since the purges of 1981, and ensured that when agreement to membership was finally exacted from Mrs Thatcher, it would be at a higher and wrong parity.

It is the quarrel and the split which matter in Machiavellian terms. The adviser was seen as too strong, too influential for other more official advisers. Ministers suspended their attempts at finding solutions in favour of the delights of a quarrel, the effects of which reverberate four years on in the government of John Major. Alan Walters was not solely responsible for the condition among ministers which made government by late 1989 come to resemble Haydn's Farewell Symphony – the one in which clarinets, bassoons, violas, double-basses, cellos and percussion, one by one, blow out their candles, pick up their music, bow to the conductor and leave, until at last one solitary violinist is left sawing away. Mrs Thatcher had some hand in that.

Walters, however, was a major part of the quarrel with Nigel Lawson and hardly a less important part of the row with Geoffrey Howe. And the departures of these two demonstrated what Machiavelli warned against in an adviser. It has been quoted above, but such is its damning aptness in the case of Mrs Thatcher that it can stand quoting again:

> But when seeking advice of more than one person, a prince who is not himself wise will never get unanimity in his councils or be able to reconcile their views . . . the conclusion is that good advice, whomever it comes from, depends on the

> shrewdness of the prince who seeks it, and not the shrewdness
> of the prince upon good advice.

Precisely, for the central flaw in Mrs Thatcher lay in her personalization of government. Instead of picking advisers, listening to them and coming to conclusions right or wrong without personal feelings, she invested her huge capacity for faction in the debate, herself determining the saved and the damned, the outer and inner, the us and the not-us. By dint of endless bullying, with remissions for gluey charm, she made government itself an immensely exhausting and emotionally wearing experience.

In the case of Lawson, she not only ground him very fine – in the manner of the mills of God – she also demonstrated on him a propensity for desertion and dropping, already visited upon a check-list of ministers across the decade. He was too big to be fired but not too big to be persecuted and being both big *and* persecuted, he went of his own accord. His going was the beginning of her going. Nothing that Lawson might be wrong about, like shadowing the D-mark, was as injurious on the reckoning of statesmen and princes as his departure.

A finance minister who resigns and makes clear that the Prime Minister has lost his confidence indicates all sorts of delightful possibilities in the political near-future. He casts doubt upon legitimacy, he opens the field of speculation. He replaces the Prime Minister as the withdrawer of love and the maker of judgements. Many pale Wildean jokes were made about the respective misfortune and carelessness of losing first a Finance Minister and then a Foreign Secretary. And with the departure of Geoffrey Howe a year later, Margaret Thatcher ended the period of speculation about *her* and began the much shorter speculation about her end.

Fundamentally, she was that prince 'who is not himself wise'. Accordingly, she got no unanimity in her councils except by fear. Her governments might, at the end, be divided into three categories of minister: worshipper, functionary and enemy. Advisers were allowed to become injurious not only through their personal folly – and Walters for one had perfected a style of naïve insolence calculated to send the mildest of men, which Lawson is not, into ceramic-smashing fury – but through her failure to restrain it. She practised an odd mixture of deviousness, fast-burning, fast-extinguished love, side-taking absolutism and ferocious contempt for those no longer useful. She never understood the self-interested arguments for behaving decently. Unwanted ministers were strictly biodegradable. It was impressive at first but long before she fell, ministers had grown to see the brevity and unreliability of her favour. In the early days, not fathoming her, they waited for changes of mood and found themselves waiting for dismissal (hers was not a love which, once extinguished, was ever relumed).

The Farewell Symphony departures were a pre-emption of her readily foreseen displeasure, a getting-out while the going is good not practised in healthy governments. She was thus, in John Clare's phrase, 'the self-consumer of her woes'. Michael Heseltine, in conflict with her over the Westland helicopter issue, a modest thing in itself, took the view, according to his friends, that a defeat would not be a matter of winning some, losing some. It would be death in the mouth of Bernard Ingham – exactly like the earlier departure of John Biffen for dissent on policy – a rubbishing of the offender by the Prime Minister's prime minister, a murmuring to the press, well ahead of his dispatch, that he was not essential or useful. Past experience informed Heseltine what he must expect and made him ready to strike first, as he did with his Technicolor departure, on-camera, clean out of a cabinet meeting. If you mean to put someone on the street, it is not wise to let it be Downing Street.

The contrast with Harold Wilson is instructive. He was a sweet-natured man, too timid, diminished by the defiance of one adviser, James Callaghan, on a central policy, damaged again less by the actions than by the advertised and heavily discussed presence of another adviser, his confidante Mrs Williams. Had Wilson been more authoritarian, he would not have suffered humiliation where he was clearly trying to do the right thing. If Mrs Thatcher had been less authoritarian, she would have had harder struggles for her early policies (and seeing what they were – a monetary squeeze followed by a fiscal one, between them producing a *low* point in unemployment of just under 1.6 millions – she would have been none the worse). But also, she would never have seen a procession of forewarned ministers registering a mute, serial and quietly aggregating vote of no personal confidence, nor seen that subsidence followed by two resignation earthquakes, neither small, in the second of which she was the only one killed.

Wilson used his outside adviser, Williams, for emotional solace, which indicates his failings as a prince. Thatcher used hers, Walters, to make war on her ministers and yet another outsider, Bernard Ingham, her press officer, to shoot them. Wilson sank beneath his own despair and resigned, weary of politics, in 1976. Thatcher, furious to devour more and enjoy further time under the lights, left in November 1990 on a tide of her party's despair. Her misuse of her advisers united the cabinet for her dispatch. Between extremes of exploitative imperiousness and fearful caution, both of which emboldened their impertinent advisers' step, Thatcher and Wilson marked opposite ends of a spectrum across which any sensible man would wish to plot a quiet, sensible path. Never have two governments given such dreadful and opposite warnings.

BIBLIOGRAPHY

Barzini, Luigi, *The Italians* (Penguin, 1991)

Bullock, Alan, *Hitler and Stalin: Parallel Lives* (HarperCollins, 1991)

Conquest, Robert, *The Great Terror* (Penguin, 1971)

Crawley, Eduardo, *A House Divided: Argentina, 1880–1980* (C. Hurst & Co., 1984)

Giles, Frank, *The Lotus Years, 1946–58, The Story of the Fourth French Republic* (Secker & Warburg, 1991)

Gilmour, Ian, *Dancing with Dogma: Thatcherite Britain in the Eighties* (Simon & Schuster, 1992)

Hibbert, Christopher, *Benito Mussolini* (Longman, 1965)
—— *Garibaldi and his Enemies* (Penguin, 1987)

Hills, George, *Franco* (Robert Hale, 1967)

Jones, Nigel H., *Hitler's Heralds* (John Murray, 1987)

Lampedusa, Giuseppe Tomasi di, *The Leopard* (Collins Harvill, 1986)

Lawson, Nigel, *The View from Number Eleven: Memoirs of a Tory Radical* (Bantam Press, 1992)

Levi, Carlo, *Christ Stopped at Eboli* (Penguin, 1990)

Morgan, Austen, *Harold Wilson: A Life* (Pluto Press, 1992)

Orwell, George, *Animal Farm* (Penguin, 1989)
—— *Nineteen Eighty-Four* (Penguin, 1989)
—— *Collected Essays* (Secker & Warburg, 1970)

Pimlott, Ben, *Harold Wilson* (HarperCollins, 1992)

Quiller-Couch, Arthur, 'Tradition and Orthodoxy', 1934; lecture reprinted in John Gross, *The Rise and Fall of the Man of Letters* (Penguin, 1991)

Sabato, Ernesto, *El Otro del Peronoismo*

Schiff, Ze'ev, and Ya'ari, Ehud, *Israel's Lebanon War* (Unwin, 1985)

Williams, Philip M., and Harrison, Martin, *De Gaulle's Republic* (Greenwood Press, 1979)

Also available

MICHAEL FOOT

by Mervyn Jones

'A book of quality about a man of qualities'
ROY JENKINS, *Daily Telegraph*

'Warming, saddening and revealing'
PETER HENNESSY, *Times Educational Supplement*

'Mervyn Jones, in this splendid book, corrects all the
myths which have grown up around the man and
presents him to the reader accurately and
sympathetically. And what a story he has to tell'
TONY BENN, *Evening Standard*

£9.99 paperback
0 575 05933 8